A Noble Example

ALSO AVAILABLE
BY EUGENE W. BAKER

Nothing Better Than This: *The Biography of James Huckins, First Baptist Missionary to Texas*

In His Traces: *The Life and Times of R. E. B. Baylor*

A Noble Example

A Pen Picture of William M. Tryon,
Pioneer Texas Baptist Preacher
and Co-Founder of Baylor University

Eugene W. Baker

BIG BEAR BOOKS

Originally published in 1985 by Baylor University, Waco, Texas 76798

Library of Congress Catalog Card Number: 85-72599
ISBN: 0-933335-01-6

New paperback ISBN: 978-1-60258-581-2

Printed in the United States of America

To

Kimberly and Michael

Foreword

Those who are interested in the early years of Baptist life in Texas will doubtless have read Z. N. Morrell's *Flowers and Fruits from the Wilderness* and Robert A. Baker's *History of the Baptist General Convention of Texas*. Eugene W. Baker now renders a notable service to Texas Baptists by supplementing these more extensive studies with a pen portrait of William M. Tryon, pioneer Texas Baptist preacher, educator, and co-founder of Baylor University and the Baptist General Convention of Texas.

I am impressed with at least three things. First, the quality of William M. Tryon's life. As missionary, evangelist, pastor, organizer, and administrator, he excelled. In every position and in all ways he was "a noble example." His excellent gifts were totally committed to Jesus Christ.

Then there is the skill with which the author has presented the main facts of Tryon's life and service. Condensation and simplification are never easy. Eugene Baker has examined letters, minutes of churches and associations, histories of educational institutions, state legislative records, state Baptist papers and many other sources of information about William M. Tryon. He has made these sources his own, and in this book has offered them in splendid form to those of us who may not have the time or opportunity to undertake such a task.

But there is more to this book than a simple pen portrait. From beginning to end we are challenged to consider the wonder of God's grace exhibited in a gifted, devoted minister of the gospel. A faith which inspired such a life can hardly be considered irrelevant in Christian education and today's world.

James H. Landes
Executive Secretary-Treasurer
Baptist General Convention of Texas
1974–1982

Preface

The cause of Christ in mid-nineteenth-century Texas lost one of its most faithful and effective servants when William Milton Tryon was felled by yellow fever on 16 November 1847, at the age of thirty-eight.

During his brief seven years as a leader of the Baptist denomination in Texas—first as a missionary of the American Baptist Home Mission Society, and then as an appointee of the Board of Domestic Missions of the Southern Baptist Convention—Tryon traveled hundreds of miles to share the Gospel of Jesus Christ. He founded numerous churches (pastoring six, several at the same time), conducted evangelistic rallies across Texas, and baptized scores of individuals. In addition to his pastoral duties he was moderator of the Union Baptist Association (five times), corresponding secretary of the Texas Home Mission Society, chaplain of the Senate during the Seventh and Eighth Congresses, treasurer of the Texas Literary Institute, and a trustee of the Houston Female Institute. He also helped organize and was an officer of the Texas Baptist Education Society, and was one of the founders of Baylor University, as well as the first president of its board of trustees.

As an orator Tryon was unparalleled in Texas, and as a persuader of men, there were few equal in the Baptist denomination in the 1840s. His love of the Savior was evident in all his endeavors, and he never sought recognition or acclaim for himself. Indeed, he felt that his place was *behind the Cross* and that the life and work of Christ should be made manifest.

The cane-brake pioneer preacher Z. N. Morrell considered himself fortunate to be the friend of Tryon, who he felt could sway the masses at will. In his classic *Flowers and Fruits from the Wilderness*, Morrell stated that Tryon was the leader in the cause of education among the Baptists in Texas. Morrell believed that Tryon's crowning achievement was his involvement in the establishment of Baylor University. This institution was first Tryon's idea, and he spent the time from its chartering in February 1845 until his death, two years and nine months later, invigorating life into the newborn limbs of what has become the world's largest Baptist university and the oldest educational institution in Texas. Morrell was convinced that Tryon's "labors of love" would never be forgotten and that every student educated in Baylor University owes him a debt of gratitude.

Undeniably, Tryon was one of the foremost leaders of early Texas Baptists. He was bold and innovative, yet compassionate and pleasant. According to Judge Robert Emmett Bledsoe Baylor, one of his colleagues and admirers, Tryon showed the mark of genius at times and had the sweetest smile and laugh of any man he ever knew.

It was to Judge Baylor that Tryon, burdened to some degree with a premonition of death, confessed that, "when he was no more," he wished "some notice of his life in Texas" would be made by those who followed. Several years after Tryon's death Judge Baylor wrote that even though it might appear that Tryon's request was influenced to some extent by an honest love of fame and honorable distinction, he felt that Tryon had a much stronger and better motive.

Knowing Tryon as he did, and having traveled side-by-side with him on horseback over the wild Texas prairies and through the shadowy forests to deliver the "good news" of Christ to those hungry for the nurture of religion, Baylor believed that Tryon

> wished no doubt that his noble example and devotedness to the cause of God might be the means of stimulating the younger and ardent ones which would follow and induce them to go and do likewise, seek out new countries, neglected fields, heathen lands and preach the unspeakable riches of the glorious gospel of our blessed Saviour Jesus Christ.

There is no visual likeness known to exist of Tryon, and only a few brief biographical sketches have made their way into print to tell his story. J. M. Carroll stated in his *A History of Texas Baptists* that

> words are absolutely inadequate justly to portray him [Tryon], whether in his personal, religious life in the pulpit, mingling among his brethren, or among the masses, as chaplain in the Texas Congress, in denominational meetings, in revivals, in councils, as pastor, as a friend or as a leader in educational work.

Though that statement is undoubtedly accurate, this small volume is a meager attempt to take "some notice of his life in Texas" for which Tryon yearned, and to paint a "pen picture" of the man and his mission in life.

e.w.b.

Acknowledgments

Assistance in the research and preparation of this volume was provided by many individuals. Special gratitude is offered to Mr. Kent Keeth, director, The Texas Collection, Baylor University, Waco, Texas, for his invaluable advice, as well as for that of his co-workers Mrs. Ellen Brown and Mr. and Mrs. William Ming. Appreciation also is expressed to Mr. Ben Rogers, archivist, The Southwestern Baptist Theological Seminary, Fort Worth, Texas, for his suggestions and research services.

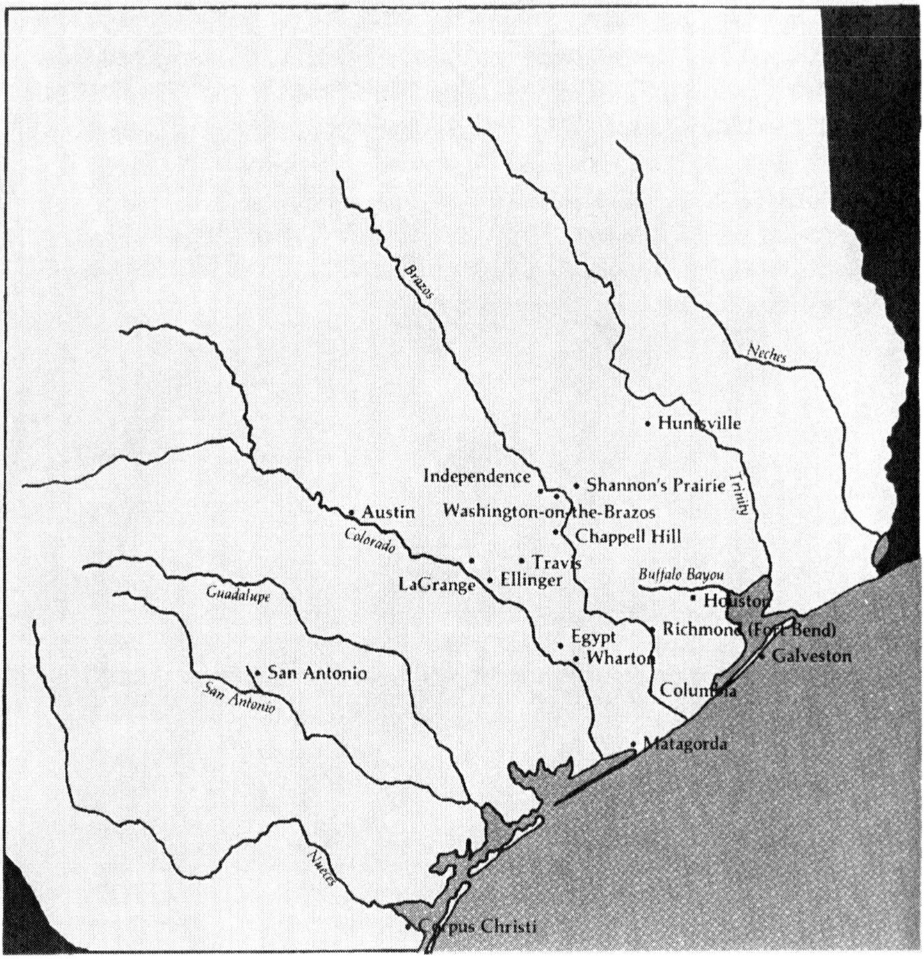
Brazos
Neches
Huntsville
Trinity
Independence
Shannon's Prairie
Austin
Washington-on-the-Brazos
Chappell Hill
Colorado
Travis
Ellinger
LaGrange
Buffalo Bayou
Houston
Guadalupe
Richmond (Fort Bend)
Egypt
Galveston
Wharton
San Antonio
San Antonio
Columbia
Matagorda
Nueces
Corpus Christi

1

IN DECEMBER 1845 the Reverend William Milton Tryon was called to become the pastor of the First Baptist Church in Houston. The small congregation of that Texas bayou city had not held regular worship services for more than two years, and although some of the members were not personally acquainted with the thirty-six-year-old minister, all were aware of his reputation and eagerly anticipated his leadership.

Tryon had lived in Texas for almost five years, and during this time he had become one of the most respected ministers in the country. He had preached throughout the republic to small and large audiences in a variety of places, including log cabins, offices, store buildings, and city halls, as well as on busy street corners, under the swooping branches of giant oak trees, and along the shores of meandering streams and rushing rivers. His missionary spirit and fervent zeal in sharing the Gospel through clear and convincing sermons had brought hundreds into the denomination's fold. Judge R. E. B. Baylor confided to the Reverend James Huckins that "Everywhere Tryon went God seemed to own and bless his labors of love."[1]

Though only of medium height and weighing a scant 130 pounds, his power of exhortation far exceeded his physical appearance. Indeed, his "clear, strong, musical, mellow voice" was the primary reason many of his colleagues claimed him to be the best preacher in Texas.[2] Tryon had an intense love for people and a great desire to lead everyone he could to Christ. His sermons rarely failed to impress his audiences, and the Reverend Z. N. Morrell wrote from his personal observation that Tryon had the uncanny ability to "exhort a guilty soul until the sinner would turn pale."[3]

Although embued with special oratorical abilities, Tryon never sought praise for these talents. In fact, he often remarked to his friends that a preacher ought to stand behind the cross of Christ and not let even his little finger be seen.[4] It was a principle in which he firmly believed and practiced.

The Baptist church in Houston had been organized in May 1841 under the leadership of the Reverend James Huckins, the first Baptist missionary appointed to Texas by the American Baptist Home Mission Society. Established in 1832 and headquartered in New York, the society existed to send missionaries and agents to various states and territories to spread the Gospel. Huckins had received his commission in 1838 and had served in South Carolina and Georgia for about a year before volunteering to visit Texas to determine the potential for mission work in the young republic.

During the first half of 1840, Huckins had traveled to many of the towns and settlements along the Texas frontier, preaching to eager crowds and baptizing scores of converts. In his report on his findings to the Mission Society that summer, he also presented a request for permission to return to Texas in order to establish a permanence for the meager Baptist work then underway there. This request had eagerly been granted by the executive committee.

Some of the most pleasant tasks undertaken by Huckins after his return to Texas had involved the leading of groups of Baptist believers to form churches. Among them were the twenty-three men and women who chartered the Houston Baptist Church.

For two years following the establishment of the Houston

church, Huckins had ministered to its members in conjunction with his pastoral responsibilities to a small congregation in Galveston, a group that he had constituted into a church in January 1840.[5] However, in 1843, because of added responsibilities — including his opening of a school for young men and women in Galveston, and his attempt to answer the "Macedonian cry" from settlements in the interior of the republic — Huckins had had to forego active preaching in Houston. Since then the congregation had dwindled from approximately two dozen members to seven, only one of whom was a male.[6] The only religious services held during the next two years were prayer meetings conducted by the Ladies Sewing Circle of the church. The members of this group were determined that the cause of Christ would not die in their city, and it was because of this resolve that William Tryon was eventually led to Houston.[7]

In mid-1845, Thomas J. Pilgrim, a noted educator who in 1829 had started the first Baptist Sunday School in Texas, went to Houston on business.[8] As was his custom on his travels around Texas, he sought Baptist believers with whom he could worship. Since the only religious activity he could find at that time was a prayer meeting of the Ladies Sewing Circle, he joined the group for meditation. Upon learning that the ladies were without a spiritual shepherd, he recommended Tryon. Later, at a conference in the home of T. B. J. Hadley, the members of the sewing circle were joined by several others from the church in issuing an invitation to William Tryon to become their pastor.[9]

The Houston church would become Tryon's sixth pastorate in Texas, but it would be the first in which he could occupy the same pulpit each Sunday. The several churches he had simultaneously served since arriving in the Lone Star Republic in January 1841 had only monthly preaching and business sessions, requiring him to conduct a circuit ministry among them.

Tryon's ministerial preparation had begun years earlier when, as a young man, he felt the call of the Lord to become a preacher. Born on 10 March 1809 in New York, William Tryon was the son of William and Jane Phillips Tryon. His mother had come to

America from England when only seven years old, and his father, a fifth-generation American, traced his ancestry back to mid-seventeenth-century England.[10] When the elder Tryon died in 1820 while in St. Louis, Missouri, on a fur-hunting expedition, William went to live with a wealthy uncle in Connecticut. Because of chronic ill health, however, he soon returned to New York. There he took up the trade of tailor to help support his mother and the younger members of his family.[11]

In his late teens he became a Christian and was baptized into the South Baptist Church in New York City by the Reverend C. G. Sommers. Some time later he went southward in search of a healthier climate, eventually moving to Augusta, Georgia, where he worked as a tailor. In December 1832 he was licensed to preach by the First Baptist Church of that city.

Educational opportunities for those interested in preparing themselves to become Baptist preachers were rare in Georgia. But, since 1822, when the Georgia Baptist Convention was established, organized attempts had been made to assist in the "education of young men whose piety and gifts for the ministry, in the judgment of their churches, indicated the Divine will that they should enter upon that important and holy service."[12]

The pastor of the First Baptist Church in Augusta, Charles D. Mallary, was an outspoken proponent of Sunday schools, foreign and domestic missions, and the education of ministers. He probably was influential in Tryon's decision to enroll in January 1833 as one of the first students at Mercer Institute in Penfield, Georgia.

The small manual-labor school had been the outgrowth of increasing interest among Georgia Baptists in ministerial education. Since 1825 money had been sporadically contributed by Baptist congregations scattered across the state. These funds were usually used to supplement salaries of ordained preachers who tutored students in their homes for specific periods of time.

In 1829, a bequest of twenty-five hundred dollars from the estate of Josiah Penfield of Savannah opened doors to new concepts and alternative ways to educate ministers. During the denomination's annual convention that year, delegates matched

Penfield's gift with contributions of their own. As a result, a permanent endowment for ministerial educational programs was established. At a state-wide gathering two years later, Baptist leaders passed a resolution that stated that "as soon as funds will justify it, this Convention will establish in some central part of the state, a literary and theological school, which shall unite manual labor with study admitting others besides students in Divinity."[13]

Shortly thereafter, a four-hundred-fifty-acre site, seven miles north of Greensboro in Green County, was purchased for $1450. The Reverend Billington Sanders was then selected as principal and steward, and the facilities — two double log cabins with garrets for dwelling, dining, and study — were soon made ready for young men, ranging from preteen to early manhood, who wanted an education.[14] The location was called Penfield in memory of the major benefactor, and the school was named in honor of the Reverend Jesse Mercer, the acknowledged leader of Georgia Baptists.

From the originally registered twenty-two students, the enrollment quickly grew to thirty-nine. Five of these, including William Tryon, were "ministerial licentiates" and beneficiaries of the Baptist Convention.

The institute was situated amidst tall, thickly growing trees. Occasional clearings provided space for the buildings and the farming operations. Most of the activities centered in one of the "halls" where the boys were summoned before sunrise every morning for roll call, devotion, and prayer. It was here that the students received the orders of the day, after which they tended to their chores until interrupted by the sound of the breakfast bell. The "eating house" contained two long tables. At the end of one sat the principal and his wife, who supervised the etiquette at meals. When all the students had filed to their seats and grace was completed, the "squadron of consumers made an onslaught upon the good things spread before them."[15]

Following breakfast in the winter months, the boys returned to their morning chores or lessons until about ten o'clock, when the ringing of the bell drew each into an assembly to receive implements with which to work in the field — some to till the soil for planting or cultivating, others to push back the forest to make room for future agricultural endeavors. They then marched in ranks and files to assigned work areas, where they toiled for three hours under the vigilant but sympathetic watch of the Reverend Sanders, who not only supervised, but also worked alongside the students to provide an example and to give assistance. At one o'clock the bell rang to call the workers to lunch.

> All at once, in the midst of flame, smoke, the sound of axes, and the shouts of the most lively fellows that bell was heard again. As by magic, and in a moment, axes, wedges, rakes, and handsticks fell from blistered hands and weary arms, as though paralysis had seized upon every muscle. The work upon the new ground was finished for that day, and every body in his own way, and by the nearest route, sought the house. They went out in solemn order — they returned in glorious and tumultuous disorder.[16]

During the warmer months, the work in the field began at seven o'clock and lasted till mid-morning, when studies were performed until the ritual race to the lunch table.

For a brief period following the meal, students were allowed free time to do as they chose, but with the renewed clanging of the bell each "scholar" was called to a period of study and recitation under the principal or his assistant teachers. This lasted until the bell beckoned them to evening prayers and supper.

After eating, the students leisurely studied by the light of tallow candles, lard lamps, or torch lights until nine o'clock, when the bell rang again to signify the end of another day.[17] The students had been up since long before daylight, and each had labored for three hours and had been engaged in some type of intellectual pursuit for approximately seven hours. It was a demanding schedule, and one that was strictly enforced, though the principal readily admitted that he had less difficulty getting the students to labor than to study.[18]

School terms were set to correspond with the best production schedule for crops, which usually consisted of corn, potatoes, peas, and cotton. The first term began in January and lasted six months. Following a week's vacation, the second term started, continuing until the Christmas holidays. The subjects included English, Greek, and Latin, as well as grammar, geography, literature, and logic. Board was approximately four dollars per month. Tryon's expenses for the first year, paid by the Georgia Baptist Convention, amounted to some sixty-five dollars.[19]

In his second year, in addition to his farming duties and normal studies, Tryon became a member of the Franklin Polemic Society. The major purpose of this organization, which had been established in January 1833, was to foster debate and discussion on selected topics. The first subject chosen for deliberation after Tryon became a member concerned the amount of pleasure attainable in married life, as compared to that in single life. In special ceremonies on Washington's birthday, Tryon teamed with his close friend Charles F. Sturgis — who later became a missionary to the Indians — to win the debate on the topic. Their choice was the single lifestyle.[20] It was, perhaps, an early indication of his ability with words.

His brilliance as a speaker and his scholarly acumen were constantly noticed by his classmates and the Reverend Sanders. Because of these recognized abilities, he was requested by the Georgia Baptist Convention's executive board to serve during his third year at Mercer as an instructor for some of the younger students. Tryon's assumption of this duty during 1835 allowed more time for the principal to direct the farm operations. For his services he was paid fifty dollars.[21]

In January 1836, following the completion of his course of study at Mercer, Tryon was appointed General Agent for the Georgia Baptist Convention at an annual salary of five hundred dollars.[22] In this capacity he traveled around the state to solicit funds for the convention's educational and missionary programs.

For a number of years there had not been agreement among Georgia Baptists on the propriety of church support of missions, Sunday schools, Bible societies, and other benevolent institutions. This lack of agreement hampered Tryon's efforts to collect money. On 7 July 1836, at Forsyth in Monroe County, Tryon joined more than fifty other ministers in a formal recognition of the autonomy of individual Baptist churches in all matters. They published a notice in which they pledged non-interference with congregations that chose to support — or not to support — missionary and educational endeavors. In addition, the ministers approved articles of faith, the first for the denomination in Alabama.[23]

The effect throughout the state was almost magical, as interest and support in the convention's programs immediately increased, especially in the permanent endowment for education, and in the building, general purpose, and Burma mission funds.[24] As a result, Tryon soon collected numerous payments on old subscriptions and garnered a considerable number of new ones.[25] Despite this sudden success and the potential for even greater results, Tryon was not content. He wanted to preach.

To be effective in the pastoral ministry, Tryon felt he needed additional education. Since the Georgia Baptist Convention had generously paid his expenses at Mercer, and had provided him employment following his studies there, Tryon assumed he could count on similar support to continue his education at the Theological Seminary in Andover, Massachusetts.

In this, however, he was disappointed, for on 6 May 1837, the convention's executive committee denied his request. They suggested that he return instead to Mercer and take special courses. If he would do so, they agreed to be responsible for his expenses.[26] Though Tryon earnestly desired to improve his theological knowledge, he did not feel additional course work at Mercer would be advantageous. He therefore abandoned his desire to return to school. The next month he accepted the pastorate of the Baptist church at Irwinton, Alabama, a small town near the Chattahoochee River.

Irwinton originally had been named Eufaula, after the Eufaula Indians of the Creek nation who had lived on the bluff overlooking the town. Around 1830, the name was changed to Irwinton in honor of state senator William Irwin, who had provided the capital for the first business enterprise in the settlement.

During the early years of its existence, Irwinton had few permanent settlers, even though steamboats continually plied the river and trade with the Indians was profitable. In 1834, numerous families moved into the community, and the next summer several hotels, taverns, and a variety of other businesses opened.[27] Within about two years, the population of Irwinton increased to some five hundred, and both a Methodist and a Presbyterian church were organized. The town gradually became a major stagecoach stop on lines running to Columbus and Fort Gaines, Georgia; Montgomery, Alabama; and Tallahassee, Florida. Because of this development, mail could be received from New York in twelve days, and merchants could order and obtain delivery of supplies from that same city within a month.[28]

In June 1837, the Baptist church that would call William Tryon as its first pastor was organized.[29] Later that summer, Tryon was ordained by the church and began his ministry in the community. His work was challenging and rewarding, but in a letter to his friend and mentor Jesse Mercer, he revealed that "wilst I have been frequently gratified at the attention and good order manifested by our congregations, I have often lamented that so little apparent good was effected."[30]

Two members of his own church and a member of the Presbyterian congregation also were dismayed because of the infrequent manifestations of spirituality. In an effort to effect some changes, these men covenanted together in the spring of 1838 to make the religious condition of Irwinton a subject of special prayer. Others gradually became similarly convicted, and, by summer, weekly prayer meetings were being held in all the Protestant churches in the town, each one crowded almost to capacity.

In August, during a two-week joint meeting of the Baptist, Methodist, and Presbyterian congregations in Irwinton, almost one hundred people made decisions to follow Christ. Thirty-six of these joined the Baptist faith. In a letter to Jesse Mercer, Tryon described his joy over the results of the revival, stating that "I never in my life before, attended a meeting where there seemed to be manifested a greater spirit of prayer, and apparently more plain answers to the supplications of God's people."[31]

These results were more than duplicated that fall at the Bethlehem Baptist Church in Barbour County, twenty-seven miles west of Irwinton. Prior to this time, the Bethlehem church, one of the oldest in that part of the state, had been declining for several years. In fact, it had almost dissolved in 1837, when many of its members left to join a church in nearby Clayton. Tryon had accepted the additional pastoral responsibility of the remaining members early in 1838 and, that spring, had performed the first baptism of his ministry at this church.[32]

During the second week of October 1838, a revival meeting was scheduled to be held at the church. Several of Tryon's minister friends who were to preach failed to arrive by the appointed evening, and Tryon had to begin the meeting by himself. Before the series of services was completed, torrential rainstorms drove the outdoor sessions into crowded and cramped quarters. These circumstances, however, failed to dampen the desire of the people or weaken the work of the spirit of the Lord, as fifty-five people were converted during a ten-day period. Because of the large number of new Christians, baptismal services had to be conducted four times during the revival. One of these observances attracted more than three hundred onlookers.[33]

The successes experienced by the Irwinton and Bethlehem congregations inspired the members of the Irwinton church to erect a permanent brick worship center.[34] In the spring of 1838, a supervising committee was formed. Construction was not started until several months later, however. During this period Tryon traveled to numerous communities across the state and led revivals in which scores of people were converted.[35]

In mid-November 1839, Tryon attended the annual Alabama Baptist Convention, which was held in Perry County. There the delegates learned of the limited success that agents of the convention were having in raising money. Tryon had heard similar news at the anniversary gathering the previous November. As a member of the Domestic Mission Committee at that time, he had joined others in publicly requesting pastors to hold frequent fund-raising activities and to solicit contributions from the general public.[36]

Unfortunately, only a few individuals had taken these suggestions seriously. As a result, very little increase in gifts had been experienced. In an effort to improve the situation, delegates to the 1839 convention voted to replace the salaried agents with volunteers. William Tryon was one of eight picked to serve in this capacity.[37]

Soon after the convention, Tryon was unanimously reelected pastor of the Irwinton Baptist church for the upcoming year. Unknown to his congregation, however, Tryon also had received an invitation from the Baptist church in Wetumpka, Alabama, to become its pastor. He weighed both opportunities and then accepted the Wetumpka position, closing a three-year ministry in southeast Alabama.

Wetumpka, located about twenty miles north of Montgomery, near the head of navigation on the Coosa and Alabama rivers, was a cotton center from which packet ships weekly transported hundreds of bales to warehouses in Mobile.[38] Some consideration had been given by Baptist leaders in 1838 to the development of a literary and theological institution there. A hundred-acre site near the town had even been purchased, but nothing definite was ever accomplished.[39]

At Wetumpka, Tryon soon met recently widowed Louisa J. Higgins. They were married on 14 April 1840 by the Reverend William Carey Crane, a close friend of Tryon's. The two men had been associated frequently in convention affairs, as well as in the Alabama Baptist Bible Society, of which both were officers.[40]

In June the Reverend James Huckins, returning from a five-month investigative tour of religious conditions in Texas, visited central Alabama to share his findings with various Baptist congregations.[41] Tryon, a couple of years younger than Huckins, had met him in May 1839, when both had participated in the eighteenth anniversary meeting of the Georgia Baptist Convention. At this convention, which was held in Richland, Georgia, Huckins represented the American Baptist Home Mission Society, and Tryon was a visiting messenger from the

Alabama Baptist Convention.[42]

It is not known if Tryon met with Huckins while he was touring Alabama during the summer of 1840, or if any correspondence was exchanged between the two regarding the religious plight of Texas. However, Tryon was no doubt aware of Huckins's views at least by late summer, when these were published in the Home Mission Society reports, along with pleas for ministers to take the Gospel to the new republic.

Sometime before fall 1840, Tryon contacted the Home Mission Society and volunteered his services. He was commissioned in November and spent the next few weeks raising money to fund his trip. On 4 January 1841, Tryon and his wife embarked on the first leg of a journey that would eventually thrust him into the mainstream of the uncharted course of the struggling Baptist denomination in Texas.

2

AFTER A STORMY OCEAN VOYAGE, William and Louisa Tryon landed in Galveston on 18 January 1841. They had expected to be directed immediately by James Huckins to the area most in need of a Christian minister.[1] Unfortunately, Huckins himself had arrived in Galveston only three weeks earlier and had been ill almost constantly since then. Because of his incapacitation, he had not been able to evaluate the needs of the areas soliciting Tryon's services. Huckins therefore suggested that Tryon journey on to Houston and wait until they could confer about any future assignment.[2]

Houston had been the capital of the Republic of Texas from April 1837 to September 1839. During this time of preeminence, hundreds of people had swarmed into it from various locations in the United States and Europe. The unique mixture of personalities with varying purposes and passions had created a city almost void of morality and culture. Only a few attempts at promoting religious concerns had been made, and most of these had been unsuccessful.

Perhaps the first sermon ever preached in Houston had been

delivered in March 1837, while it was still largely a city of tents. It was given by the Reverend Z. N. Morrell, the rugged pioneer Baptist preacher who had arrived in Texas in December 1835 amidst the frantic eastward flight of so many Texas residents who were beginning to flee from the threat of a Mexican invasion. Morrell's preaching drew an attentive crowd, but its novelty soon wore off, and most of the people returned to their own personal interests with little more thought of spiritual matters.[3]

The transfer of the seat of government to the frontier settlement of Austin in late 1839, coupled with devastating epidemics of yellow fever that year and the next, severely taxed the determination and pioneer resilience of Houston's inhabitants. In spite of the odds they fought back, and by January 1841, though the city's religious condition had improved only slightly, its economic prospects appeared promising.[4]

Tryon stayed in Houston for about two weeks before Huckins was well enough to visit him to discuss suitable locations for the start of his ministry.[5] Baptists in both Matagorda and Independence had requested Tryon's services. After careful consideration, Huckins and Tryon agreed that Independence offered the best opportunity.

Established in 1824 by John P. Cole, Independence was a small farming community in Washington County, north of Houston. It had been known as Coles Settlement until 1836, when the name was changed during the patriotic fever surrounding Texas' successful revolution against Mexico. The town had been the site of the first girls' school in Texas, and shortly after Texas had become an independent country, a charter had been granted by its Congress for an academy to be established in the town.[6]

In addition to the Independence Academy, which was still operating and enjoying remarkable success in 1841, the community also was the home of several prominent Texans and the location of one of the few Baptist churches in the republic. The Independence Baptist Church had been established in September 1839 by the Reverend Thomas Spraggins, while he was visiting Texas from Mississippi. During the previous year, the small church had been pastored by the Reverend Thomas W. Cox, a leading Baptist minister who had moved from Alabama in late 1838.[7]

It took about two weeks for Tryon and his wife to prepare for the horseback journey to their new place of service. The trip from Houston to Independence, normally sixty-five to seventy miles, was greatly lengthened because numerous streams and creeks had been flooded by recent rains and had thus become impassable barriers. The circuitous route by which the Tryons were forced to proceed took them to the village of Washington-on-the-Brazos, about a dozen miles from Independence. On the outskirts of that community they stopped at the home of William Bledsoe, a relative of James Huckins. Leaving his wife there, Tryon continued into town to ascertain the feasibility of his preaching there the next day, which was Sunday.

Because of the rowdy prosperity during its recent bid to become the capital city, Washington-on-the-Brazos normally was not receptive to preachers. Indeed, it was well known that most attempts at religious awakening within the community during the past few years had met with poor reception. Its few hundred citizens were just beginning to overcome the climate of depression and anger, induced some eighteen months earlier when the Texas Congress had denied the town's petition to become the permanent capital of the republic.

The coastal town of Columbia, the first seat of government after Texas had become an independent nation, had proved wholly inadequate. As a result, several cities had made bids to become the new home of the government. Among them was Washington-on-the-Brazos, which proclaimed its central location, healthy climate, fresh springs, and potential for navigation on the Brazos River as unique advantages for governmental operations. Many of the townsfolk felt that the Congress would choose to locate there, but in a close vote Houston had been named the new capital.

In mid-1839, when dissatisfaction over inadequate facilities in Houston peaked, the cry for another site was raised. Once again, Washington-on-the-Brazos made its bid to become the seat of the government. As on the first occasion two years earlier, the town's petition was denied. The commissioners who were appointed to choose the site for the new capital selected instead the immature community of Waterloo on the Colorado River. The name subsequently was changed to Austin, and a fourteen-block square was immediately laid out to welcome the Fourth Congress, which was scheduled to convene in November 1839.

During 1838 and early 1839, while proposed sites for the government headquarters were being investigated, Washington-on-the-Brazos had taken on an aura of prosperity in anticipation of favorable consideration. Several businesses had opened, merchants had begun advertising new wares, and numerous professional men had opened offices. The influx of scores of people into the town had created an unusually raw atmosphere, as many of the new residents sought excitement and entertainment through drinking, gambling, and horse racing. Only a small number appeared to seek the refuge of religion.

In the fall of 1837, Z. N. Morrell became the first Baptist preacher to conduct worship services in the town. His efforts met with only mild success, but they were enough to generate within the few Baptists of the community an earnest desire to unite together as a church. As a result, Morrell organized this small group into the Washington Baptist Church in November 1837. The congregation soon appointed a special committee to write letters to the Baptist mission leadership in the United States, calling for preachers to venture to Texas before "the feeble light in the wilderness" was blown out.[8]

The American Baptist Home Mission Society had attempted to appoint Morrell to carry the evangelistic torch into the scattered homesites of the republic, but his health would not permit him to accept. Though Baptists in the United States were highly interested in the mission prospects in Texas, the society had no one else immediately available to assign to the young republic, and the flame of the Baptist faith in Texas began to flicker.

By the end of 1839, it had become obvious that Austin would be the Texas capital, at least through the presidency of Mirabeau B. Lamar, which would last until December 1841. As a result, many of the citizens of Washington-on-the-Brazos became discouraged and left, eventually causing the virtual collapse of the Baptist church that Morrell had started. Of the people who remained in the town, the most boisterous received the greater amount of public attention, gradually earning for Washington-on-the-Brazos a reputation as one of the most wicked places in the country. In 1840, when James Huckins had investigated the religious conditions in Texas on behalf of the Home Mission Society, he had discovered that Washington-on-the-Brazos was indeed conforming to this reputation.

In spite of such a discouraging background, Tryon still felt impressed to preach to the people there, though he was not certain how to create such an opportunity.[9] Tryon reported later in the *Baptist Advocate* how, arriving in the town late Saturday afternoon, he hesitated only momentarily before approaching several men gathered in front of one of the stores. He announced to them his desire to preach, and to his amazement they received him cordially. One of the men even escorted him to the house of Thomas Cartness, a former member of the Baptist church in Nashville, Tennessee. Through the efforts of Cartness and a few others, arrangements were made for worship services to be held the next day.[10] It was the first spark of the flame of religious revival which soon would glow all over southeastern Texas.

After preaching at Washington-on-the-Brazos on Sunday morning, Tryon continued to Independence, where he was greeted by Thomas W. Cox, pastor of the Baptist church there. Cox lived sixty miles away, and over the months of his pastorate he had found it difficult to preach regularly at Independence. He was enthusiastic over Tryon's assignment, and readily agreed to become co-pastor of the church, giving Tryon full responsibility to take charge.[11]

Tryon soon made his residence at Hidalgo Bluff, about midway between Independence and Washington-on-the-Brazos. During the next few weeks, he preached in both these towns as well as in the surrounding communities. On the second Sunday in March, Tryon went to Washington-on-the-Brazos in an effort to rekindle the spirit of the Baptists living there and to reconstitute the church, which had practically disappeared.

Joining him as a member of the presbytery was District Judge Robert Emmett Bledsoe Baylor.

A native of Kentucky, the forty-eight-year-old Baylor had emigrated in December 1839 from Alabama, where he had lived for almost twenty years. While in Alabama he had practiced law, served as a state legislator, and been a member of the United States House of Representatives in the Twenty-first Congress. Baylor had heard Tryon preach in Alabama, and although not a Christian at that time, he recalled later that he "was struck with the force of his sermon and set him down as no ordinary man."[12]

Baylor had been converted only a short while before arriving in Texas, and now was an ordained minister who attempted to share Christ across the republic while dispensing justice in his capacity as a judge. He had operated a small school at La Grange before Congress elected him a district judge in January 1841. Baylor attended the Baptist church in Rutersville, which the Reverends James Huckins and Thomas W. Cox had constituted in 1840. He probably was the best known of all Baptists in Texas.

Tryon and Baylor reorganized the Washington Baptist Church with twelve members, two of whom were slaves. The small congregation then elected Anderson A. Buffington as clerk and James L. Farquhar as deacon. Buffington had been one of the members when Z. N. Morrell established the church. Farquhar, a native of South Carolina, had arrived from Mississippi two years earlier.[13] Following its reorganization, the church elected Tryon as its pastor. He agreed to meet with the members monthly.

During the next several weeks, Tryon visited many other communities to share the Gospel. Among these were Matagorda, where he spent two weeks, and La Grange, where, assisted by Baylor, he administered his first "Lord's Supper" or holy communion in Texas.[14] One of his greatest joys during this period occurred when he baptized his wife. She formerly had been a Methodist, but had been considering changing denominations even before leaving Alabama.[15] As the Baptists did not recognize baptisms of other denominations, it was necessary for her to be immersed in order to be accepted into the Baptist clan.

By the end of May, Tryon was conducting a multi-community circuit ministry. He preached at least once a month at Independence, Washington-on-the-Brazos, Tiger Point, and Travis, and held frequent mid-week services at other locations. He had come to Texas to share the Gospel, and he lost very few opportunities to do so.

R. E. B. Baylor once remarked to James Huckins that during Tryon's first few months in Texas the fashionable clothes he wore were sometimes a disadvantage since many to whom he attempted to minister "were badly clad at that period seeking homes . . . untenanted solitudes of nature."[16] Gradually, however, Tryon's black cloak became frazzled and torn as he spurred his Spanish pony through the briars and thickets to carry the Gospel, and as a result he became better accepted.[17] It appears that the poorer the condition of his garments, the richer the response of his audiences.

In his preaching Tryon showed unusual earnestness, and seldom did he fail to move his audiences and leave a lasting impression upon their minds. According to some of his contemporaries, his delivery was smooth and fluent and his argument clear and convincing. His appeals were normally powerful and when "wrought up" were almost overwhelming.[18]

Tryon had a good knowledge of the Bible, and his pleasant smile often made people feel that the love he expressed came right from his heart. His gestures in the pulpit were simple and natural, though he frequently was emotional to the point of tears. Of all his talents, the one most admired by colleagues was his ability to interweave into his discourses various incidents that had occurred in his own experience, and those that had been communicated to him by others. He accomplished this with graceful facility and surprising effect. Tryon's evangelistic style of preaching appealed to the religious hunger in his audiences, and often caused and sustained enthusiastic and responsive revivals. It was this very aspect of his ministry that occupied his mind and heart during his first summer in Texas.[19]

Since March, when the Washington-on-the-Brazos church

had been reorganized, several members had continued in prayer for an outpouring of the Holy Spirit.[20] The answer to these prayers came during the last week of July, when Tryon, R. E. B. Baylor, and A. A. Buffington assembled in the town to hold a weekend meeting.

The first service, held on Saturday afternoon, was led by Buffington, who only recently had decided to become a preacher. In this meeting a young slave girl was saved. She was baptized by Tryon the next morning in the waters of the Brazos River, which ran near the church.[21] The baptismal ceremony was followed by another period of worship, this one led by Baylor. That afternoon Tryon preached and issued an invitation to all who desired the prayers of God's people. Practically the entire audience of one hundred accepted this offer. "Deep feeling pervaded the assembly; and very many with streaming eyes, manifested that their hearts were affected." One man, who had "done more than any other individual to ruin the population of the place by his lawless conduct, wept like a child."[22]

The emotion was electrifying, and Tryon sensed the Holy Spirit working among the people. However, his wife was ill at the home of a friend more than twenty miles away, and he felt his presence was required there with her. Gaining assurance from Baylor that he would lead the prayer session scheduled that evening, Tryon left to join his wife. Because it was so late when he began his journey, he did not travel very far before darkness forced him to stop. As he renewed his journey the next morning, he was overtaken by Buffington who delivered the news that two more people had been saved during the evening prayer period. Buffington also informed him that many others were expressing serious interest in Christianity, and that everone felt Tryon should return to lead this religious movement.[23]

Hesitating only briefly, Tryon rode back with Buffington to the assembly grounds where the people were gathered. At that afternoon's service another person was converted. He and the two who had accepted Christ during the prayer meeting of the previous evening were scheduled to be baptized that night.

When the congregation met at the candlelit courthouse for brief devotions before the administration of the ordinance of baptism, yet another lady came forward to express her acceptance of Christ. Then "the church and congregation, singing the songs of Zion, marched in procession to the river, where, after prayer by brother Baylor," Tryon baptized the four candidates.[24] The crowd then returned to the courthouse to continue in worship, during which three more people were converted. The presence of the Lord was evident to Tryon, but he still felt the urgency of being with his sick wife. He therefore again solicited Baylor's assistance, requesting the judge to remain in the town and conduct nightly meetings, so that Tryon could go to his wife's bedside. By the time Baylor concluded the services the next Sunday, thirty-one persons had accepted Christ.[25]

Deacon James Farquhar was so impressed with the outcome of this series of meetings that he wrote to the editor of the Kentucky-based *Baptist Banner and Western Pioneer* newspaper to inform him of the events. In his letter he declared that even though he was not personally acquainted with the editor, "when the Lord displays his power in the conviction and conversion of sinners in such a manner, who could withhold from praising his name." He also emphasized that "it would have astonished the unbelieving world to have heard the statements of those who had been previously leaders in infidelity."[26]

News of the revival quickly spread across Texas, and accounts of it were even published in several Baptist papers in the United States. The report was that "vice had left the place, and that the whole population of the place was to be found in the house of prayer, crying for mercy."[27]

The revival spirit that had been ignited at Washington-on-the-Brazos rapidly extended into the surrounding communities. The next Sunday, Tryon baptized five converts at the Independence Baptist Church. This was followed by a week-long meeting in a nearby village, where Tryon and Baylor led twenty-one to accept Christ. A protracted meeting was then conducted by Tryon at the Mt. Gilead Baptist Church at Tiger Point, where greater results were obtained.[28]

Within a six-week period during July and August, more than eighty people were converted through Tryon's ministry. Because of these remarkable results, Baptists in other parts of Texas began requesting his services to lead revivals in their towns. One of these groups was in Milam County, where Tryon went in September to constitute the Providence Baptist Church. On that occasion he baptized twenty-seven, many of whom had been saved a short time earlier under A. A. Buffington's preaching. On Tryon's return to the Providence church the following month, thirteen more were converted and baptized.

Tryon originally had been commissioned by the Home Mission Society to preach but six months in the republic before returning to Alabama to raise money for the society. He had been granted a temporary extension to help reap the spiritual harvest during the summer, but now, impressed by the receptiveness of the people and the evidences of their spiritual hunger, Tryon decided to settle permanently in Texas. He therefore petitioned the executive committee of the society in the early fall to make Texas his only field of service. Since his appointment as a missionary in November 1840, he had traveled more than 1,200 miles, had preached 151 sermons, and had baptized 137 individuals. His request was enthusiastically endorsed by the society.[29]

Because he had planned initially to stay in Texas but a few months, Tryon had left several business concerns in abeyance in Alabama. Notable among these was the issue of the slaves that his wife had acquired through her first husband's estate. Realizing that his salary from the Home Mission Society and the small contributions from the several congregations he pastored would not be sufficient for his needs, Tryon decided to use the slaves for farming operations on the acreage he had purchased at Hidalgo Bluff. Therefore, in late October 1841, he sailed for the United States to settle his affairs in Alabama, and to make arrangements to bring back the slaves. About two months later, Tryon returned to Texas with the expectation of serving Christ there the rest of his life.[30]

3

SHORTLY AFTER TRYON returned from Alabama an event occurred that uniquely affected the lives of the people of Texas. Annexation of Texas to the United States had been a dream on both sides of the Sabine River almost as soon as Stephen F. Austin had led his colonists into Mexican territory in the early 1820s. The dust had barely settled from the San Jacinto battlefield, where Sam Houston's forces defeated a much larger Mexican body on 21 April 1836, before annexation fever invaded the political halls of many of the eastern states.

Not everyone, of course, was enthusiastic over annexation. Quite a few believed that any formal linkage of Texas to the United States would lead to war with Mexico, which had not yet officially recognized the independence of the Lone Star Republic. These fears were proven valid in the first week of March 1842. On that occasion, General Rafael Vasquez led several hundred Mexican soldiers into San Antonio, easily capturing the frontier city. He then sent to Refugio and Goliad detachments who quickly raised the Mexican standard over these towns.[1] Though they retreated beyond the Rio Grande a few days later, the Mexicans had succeeded in raising in many people fears reminiscent of those that had led to the "run-away scrape" — an incident six years earlier, in which many frightened Texans had rushed toward the safety of Louisiana just ahead of Santa Anna's army. For many others, however, the Vasquez raid served only to raise their anger, and caused the quick formation of volunteer military groups. These "militia" bands rushed to San Antonio, unaware that Vasquez's troops had already returned to their own country.

For several weeks normal activities in Texas were disrupted as the people prepared against the possibility of future attacks. Vasquez's raid was not the signal of an impending full-scale war, as feared by some and hoped by a few who wanted a retaliatory invasion of Mexico. Rather, it was a less-than-subtle attempt to impugn the freedom being enjoyed by the Texans. It also was Santa Anna's revenge for the expedition that Texas President Mirabeau B. Lamar had sent to Santa Fe the previous year. The purpose of that expedition had been to establish trade agreements, and to encourage the inhabitants of Santa Fe to reject Mexican authority and form an alliance with Texas. The men of this poorly planned (and even more poorly executed) expedition had easily been captured and taken as prisoners to Mexico City. Most were still incarcerated, languishing in deplorable conditions while awaiting their fates.

For a long period of time after the Mexican raid, most people in Texas seemed to be more concerned over their personal welfare and immediate protection than about religious blessings and eternal safety. Tryon, however, refused to permit these unsettled conditions to deter him from his spiritual tasks. He continued to preach regularly to the various congregations that he pastored, often baptizing new converts at each location.

At the Mt. Gilead church in Tiger Point, one of the persons he baptized was Eli Mercer, cousin of Jesse Mercer, who had participated in Tryon's ordination in 1837. Eli Mercer also was the father of Penelope Borden, wife of Gail Borden, Jr. The Bordens had become the first people baptized in the Gulf of Mexico west of the Mississippi River, when James Huckins had performed the ordinance in January 1840.[2]

Mercer had emigrated with his family to Texas in 1829, and had become one of the first producers of sugar in the country. During the fight against Mexico, he had been instrumental in organizing the militia from the jurisdiction of San Felipe de Austin, and also had supplied the Texas Army with beef and other provisions.[3] Tired of waiting for the organization of a Baptist church in his hometown of Egypt, Mercer rode horseback sixty miles to Tiger Point to be baptized by Tryon. Following the ceremony, Mercer united with the Mt. Gilead congregation, and then journeyed back to Egypt.[4]

During the first week of May 1842, Tryon joined R. E. B. Baylor, Hosea Garrett, and Elias Rogers in constituting the Providence Baptist Church in east central Washington County.[5] Garrett had arrived in Texas from South Carolina only three months earlier, and planned to remain in Texas to farm and preach. Rogers was also from South Carolina, but was only visiting the republic for a brief time. The charter members of the Providence church, numbering about a dozen, decided to hold worship services on the second Sunday of every month, with the preceding Saturday set aside for the conduct of business. They requested Tryon to become their pastor. He accepted, adding this to his other responsibilities at Independence, Washington-on-the-Brazos, and Tiger Point, along with the Travis Church in Austin County which he co-pastored with R. E. B. Baylor.

Tryon was frustrated because he had pastoral responsibilities at so many churches, and voiced this in the *Baptist Advocate.* He was willing to do it, however, because he felt if he did not, the communities would be left entirely destitute of religious guidance since there were no other preachers available to serve them.[6]

Tryon recognized that the revivals that he had led since being in Texas had been started by people — sometimes just a few — who had made a specific cause the central focus of their prayers. He therefore requested the executive committee of the American Baptist Home Mission Society to make Texas a special object of prayer of the society.[7] He wanted the Baptists of America to place Texas first in their hearts, because he was convinced that the religious destitution of the people there warranted such special attention.

During July, as Tryon was delivering the Gospel to different congregations, political activities were developing in Houston that would add another dimension to his ministry before the end of the year.

When Sam Houston had become president of the republic for the second time in December 1841, he wanted to move the seat of government from Austin back to the city which bore his name. The unanticipated invasion of Vasquez in March 1842 had given him the opportunity he sought.

Though many clamored for a retaliatory invasion into Mexico, President Houston refused to permit it. Instead, he called for a special session of Congress to discuss the situation. Using the excuse that Austin probably would not be safe for the congressmen should the Mexican marauders return, he called for the legislators to convene in Houston. When they gathered there the last week of June, the determination of a proper response to the Mexican attack was the only official item on the agenda. However, the selection of an official capital became the major item of discussion.

When the legislators adjourned near the end of July, no decision had been made on a new home for the government offices. However, because of the drastic shortcomings of Houston, many people advised the President that if the site for the future capital were not away from the bayou city, there might be a boycott of future legislative sessions by some lawmakers. Since this would be detrimental to the conducting of affairs of state, Houston reluctantly selected Washington-on-the-Brazos as the site for the Congress to gather in November for its next term. The small town was more centrally located than either Houston or Austin, was closer to populated areas that could lend protection in the event of another Mexican attack, and had an unusually good climate, with only rare cases of malaria or yellow fever. The rich red clay soil of Washington County was particularly good for farming, and its abundant groves of post oak and elm trees were inviting to the growing lumbering industry. In addition, the quality of life in the town had greatly improved recently. This was primarily due to the revivals held there the previous summer by Tryon, Baylor, and Buffington.

The wisdom of the selection of Washington-on-the-Brazos was proven in September, when Mexican military forces again invaded Texas territory, this time in greater strength than on their March intrusion. Led by General Adrian Woll, more than a thousand soldiers marched into San Antonio and took control, capturing several prominent citizens in the process. As news of the disaster spread across the republic, eager bands of militia rushed to the scene to drive the invaders back across the border. Because of the usual communication delays, the residents of Washington County did not receive word of the invasion for almost a week. When they did learn of the Mexican actions, practically every man and boy of fifteen or over made preparations to retaliate. Two days later most of the men in the county, including William Tryon, headed for the frontier.[8] What part, if any, Tryon played in the ensuing military activity is not known, for by the time the men from Washington County had arrived, the major confrontation of the opposing forces had already taken place in the Battle of Salado Creek. This skirmish, which resulted in sixty Mexican losses, led to General Woll's decision to retire south of the Rio Grande.

After it became evident that immediate danger from the Mexicans was no longer preeminent, the volunteers gradually drifted back to the various towns and communities from which they had come. The news they delivered of the Mexican retreat was joyously received, but to be on the safe side, most people remained on guard and in readiness for possible future invasions.

In November, when the members of Congress were scheduled to begin their deliberations at Washington-on-the-Brazos, the tensions caused by the Mexican attack had not yet died. In fact, it took more than two weeks after the official convening date for the Senate to muster enough members to form a quorum. The uncertainties caused by General Woll accounted for much of the delay. However, a more probable cause was general dissatisfaction with President Houston.

When the Seventh Congress finally settled down for business, early on the agenda was the election of officers, one of which was that of chaplain. Since the First Congress had met in Columbia in October 1836, the post of chaplain had been filled by well-respected ministers. Sometimes the selection of a particular individual over another was determined more by the proximity of the minister's home to the seat of government than by his unique qualifications.

In most cases, the House and the Senate elected separate individuals, but occasionally the chaplain for one house would pray in the other. In the Seventh Congress, for unknown reasons, the House of Representatives did not elect a chaplain at all. Though the senators never formally held an election, they did request Tryon to open their proceedings with prayer whenever it was convenient for him to do so.[9]

The fact that he lived near Washington-on-the-Brazos was undoubtedly a contributing factor in his selection, but probably more important was the high regard in which he was held by those in the community. Another determining factor may have been that there was no money available to pay a preacher for his services as chaplain. Tryon, who owned approximately two thousand acres in Washington County and had more than a half dozen slaves, was by no means considered wealthy, but the legislators knew that the lack of a salary for the chaplain's services would not deter him from accepting the responsibility.[10]

Tryon considered the leading of prayer in the Senate important, but he was more concerned about his role in leading the people of Texas into the kingdom of God. He believed that the lingering fear of a Mexican invasion and its disruption of everyday life greatly increased the need for his ministry, and he wanted to serve as many people in the republic as he could reach. He was able, though, to meet and to pray with the senators when his pastoral duties permitted — fourteen times before Congress adjourned in mid-January 1843.[11]

Following the legislative sessions, Tryon devoted his time to his several congregations, gradually leading many to return to the level of spiritual concern he had witnessed previous to General Woll's invasion. Although Tryon exulted in the deepened interest in religion experienced by several in his congregations, in his report to *The Religious Herald* he lamented the low number of people actually converted.[12]

In the early spring, Tryon traveled to several outlying communities to preach. In the small town of Egypt he was the second Baptist ever to deliver a sermon. While in that community, he heard about a family that had accepted salvation without the benefit of exhortation by a minister. This unusual occurrence had resulted from the reading of the New Testament, which they had cut apart and divided equally among the family members. Through the reading of the Scriptures and discussions, the parents and their two children had all been saved.[13]

When Tryon preached at a camp meeting in La Grange, many people journeyed great distances to hear him. For some it was the first sermon they had heard since coming to Texas.[14] At this meeting, Tryon became acquainted with the families of many of the men who had fought under the command of Captain Nicholas Dawson, and who had been massacred upon their surrender to General Woll's troops. In addition to those who had died, many other Fayette County militiamen had been captured and were still in prison in Mexico.

Though the subject of death did not overly occupy his thoughts, Tryon graphically encountered it during the first half of 1843, as he was called upon to conduct funerals for several members of his churches. Subjects that probably did enter often into his thoughts during this period were those of slavery and the policies of the Home Mission Society regarding appointment of slave-holding missionaries. Both Tryon and his fellow missionary James Huckins were slave owners, and as such figured prominently in the issue.[15]

Differences of opinion regarding slavery had existed for several decades, though the flare-ups had become more frequent in recent years. Many of the anti-slavery movements in the United States were overtly religious, and Baptists often were prominently involved. Efforts within the denomination to decrease the toleration of the institution of slavery had led to the formation of the American Baptist Anti-Slavery Convention in

1840. The actions of this body frequently antagonized pro-slavery groups within the denomination.[16] By mid-1841, it appeared that both the pro-slavery and anti-slavery sides were prepared to battle to protect their particular viewpoints, but skillful sidestepping and compromise averted any major rifts at that time.

The issue had refused to die, however, and by early 1843 a major division of opinion occurred again — this time over the propriety of a slave-owner being an appointee of the Home Mission Society. Editorials and news articles in various Baptist publications frequently discussed this subject, often commenting on the slaveholding status of Tryon and Huckins. Most of the remarks from the northern Baptists were critical of the two Texas missionaries. Rebuttals by their compatriots in the South argued that slave ownership had nothing to do with qualifications or effectiveness in preaching the word of God.

Attempts were made by Baptists in both the North and the South to force the Home Mission Society's executive committee to establish a formal policy that either permitted or prohibited the appointment of slave-owners as missionaries. The leaders of the society constantly vacillated in making such a policy, preferring instead to avoid the issue with a literal intrepretation of the constitution of the organization. Since this document had failed to consider the subject of slavery, they indicated that no policy could or should be developed regarding the issue. In spite of this attempt to be neutral, the society was perceived by many in the South to be antipathetic to the commissioning of slave-owners.

As a result of the spotlight focused on him by the controversy during the first few months of 1843, James Huckins tendered his resignation, hoping thereby to reduce the tension within the denomination over the issue. Tryon's feelings on the subject are unknown, but he made no such concession and remained under active appointment.[17]

The attention that Tryon received because of the quarrel in the denomination had no apparent effect on the respect shown him by his colleagues, many of whom also owned slaves. Nor did it prevent the Texas senators from unanimously electing him as chaplain in December 1843 — and this time funds were available to pay for his services. During the next seven weeks, he opened the sessions of the Texas senators forty-one times, for which he received $132.[18]

Though he stayed close to Washington-on-the-Brazos while the Eighth Congress was in session, after its adjournment in the first week of February 1844, he began to travel again. In the next several months he would cover more than six hundred miles, preaching fifty sermons, delivering forty speeches, and participating in twenty church conferences for business and prayer.

During a ten-day period in June, Tryon, Hosea Garrett, and A. G. Haynes conducted a series of meetings in three widely separated areas of the republic. Garrett was a farmer and preacher, and Haynes was deacon of Independence Baptist Church. To reach the various communities, the three men rode more than a hundred miles, crossing over rolling countryside, fording streams, and passing through dense forests. They delivered the word of God to eager crowds gathered in buildings, in brush arbors, and along the banks of rivers. Their reception was unprecedented, and scores of people were converted. Many had waited for years to hear a Baptist preacher. The grueling schedule practically exhausted Tryon, who suffered greatly from the heat.

In spite of his discomfort Tryon followed this expedition with similar ones which lasted through the summer and early fall. At a meeting in Montgomery County, he had the joy of baptizing A. H. Morrell, son of the Reverend Z. N. Morrell. The younger Morrell had recently returned from Mexico, where he had been incarcerated at the castle of Perote by General Woll. While there he had been converted and had promised the Lord that, if he made it back to Texas, he would unite with a church as soon as possible.[19]

In October 1844, Tryon participated in the anniversary meeting of the Sabine Baptist Association. The meeting was held in Harrison County in extreme northeastern Texas. The association of nine churches had a membership of approximately 250, more than 100 of whom had joined the Baptist faith by baptism during the past year.

While on the 250-mile horseback journey to Harrison County, Tryon eagerly anticipated renewing fellowship with the Reverend George F. Heard. A fellow minister with whom Tryon had worked closely in Georgia and Alabama, Heard had moved to Texas the previous fall. About a mile from where Tryon had expected to meet Heard, he passed over a small elevation that once had been the site of an Indian village. There, in the shade of a few trees Tryon discovered the grave of his dear friend. Several times during the five-day conference, Tryon returned to the grave site to meditate and to weep.[20]

On his trip to the Sabine Association, Tryon had passed through numerous communities and had preached to persons seldom visited by Baptist ministers.[21] On his return journey, he took advantage of additional opportunities to share the Gospel. At St. Augustine, Nacogdoches, and Huntsville he conducted series of services, and in Montgomery County he assisted Z. N. Morrell in constituting the Post Oak Grove Baptist Church.[22] There seemed to be a special anxiousness in Tryon's efforts. He had seen and heard of many who had a deep thirst for Baptist preaching, and he wanted above all else to meet this need.[23]

Since arriving in Texas nearly four years earlier, Tryon had been called to pastor five different congregations. He had constituted several churches, traveled hundreds of miles to preach, and had baptized more than two hundred people. That was only a beginning, however, for shortly before the end of 1844, Tryon would report to the Home Mission Society that even yet the "harvest here, is indeed great."[24]

4

SINCE HIS DAYS as an assistant instructor at Mercer Institute, William Tryon had been an ardent advocate of education and a firm believer in the benefits of assiduous application to study. A passionate student of the Bible and an authority on Baptist history, Tryon frequently encouraged others to expand the limits of their knowledge. When absent from his home on journeys, he invariably assigned his wife lessons in history, mythology, and literature, and expected her to have them completed prior to his return.[1]

Tryon, of course, was but one of many in Texas who had an abiding interest in education. This subject had had an ever-increasing importance since the mid-1820s, when Stephen F. Austin's colonists had begun to overcome the challenges of their physical environment sufficiently to consider educational options for their children. The earliest attempts at formal education had usually been simple ones — often rude log cabins built by families upon their farms in which they engaged wandering scholars to teach their own and their neighbors' children.[2] Others taught their offspring in their own homes, and still others sent their sons and daughters to one of the few private or church-related schools as these gradually came into existence.

Not all people in Texas felt that children should receive a formal education. Some believed that the best learning came from household chores or field work. This approach was not unnatural for persons who were attempting to eke out their existence from a relentless frontier, but fortunately it was not the predominant attitude of the population. In fact, the failure of the Mexican government to provide an appropriate system of public education had formed one of the main complaints registered by the Texas colonists in their 1836 declaration of independence.

After Texas had obtained its freedom from Mexico in the spring of 1836, the new nation's Congress might have been expected to feel under some obligation to develop a system of popular education. This was not the case, however. Indeed, the cause seemed to have been forgotten, or at least greatly neglected at the time, by most of the lawmakers. Eventually, though, they did charter a few private institutions. Almost two and a half years would pass before any legislation would appear in support of education. The first was in January 1839, when the Congress enacted a law that set aside three leagues of land in each county for the establishment of a primary school or academy.[3] The next year the requirement for an additional league was legislated. Though the sale of these lands was intended to provide a financial foundation for the initiation of a system of public education, the actual revenues proved insufficient for this cause. Land was so cheap in the republic that even the sale of these huge acreages failed to generate the income necessary to fund any type of public school system.

As a result, most institutions established in the republic were private or church-related. Though variously named academies, institutes, seminaries or universities, each taught the basic rudimentary subjects. The schools bearing "university" or "collegiate" titles usually offered more courses at higher levels than the others, which were normally thought of as preparatory schools. A collegiate institution was felt to add prestige to the community in which it was located, and most citizens were desirous of having a school of this kind nearby.

Although the Texas Congress chartered a host of schools, the founders of many educational institutions did not seek charters, or even feel the need for them. Instead, they relied on the good faith and reputation of their instructors, administrators, and trustees to gain the support of their proposed constituents.

The first college in Texas that experienced real success was Rutersville College, established in 1840 by the Methodists. Not until October 1844 did the Baptist denomination take any significant strides into the educational arena. When they did so, William Tryon, a principal promoter of the cause since his arrival in the country, was among the leaders of the movement.

In October 1841, nine Baptist churches from seven counties gathered at the Clear Creek meeting house near Rutersville for the first anniversary of the Union Baptist Association. Tryon, having just completed the most successful series of revivals ever held in the history of the republic, was elected moderator of the organization. R. E. B. Baylor was elected corresponding secretary, the post to which he had been elected at the inaugural conference the previous year.[4]

On the second day of the meeting, Baylor made his secretarial report, a portion of which concerned education. It referred to the formation of a society to sponsor the development of a denominational institution. The idea for this proposal had originated with Tryon, who had discussed it with Baylor, perhaps during one of the many occasions when they had conducted revival meetings during the spring and summer. Baylor was wholeheartedly in agreement with the plan, and his report indicated his approval.[5] The next day Tryon appointed James Huckins, W. H. Ewing of Washington church, and a Mr. Green as a committee to consider the feasibility of the proposal.

Later that morning, the standing Committee on Education recommended the formation of an education society. They further encouraged all the people there to unite in the promotion of its work.[6] The association's minutes record that this recommendation was adopted, but the minutes also note that a similar resolution was later presented by the three-member committee appointed by Tryon. The proposal of that group also suggested that an education society be formed, and invited everyone to become members of it.[7] Whether these were different committees — the standing committee on the one hand, and another composed of the special appointees — is not clear. The individual who recorded the minutes may simply have repeated himself. Regardless, the association approved the establishment of what would become known as the Texas Baptist Education Society. Presumably, this body was organized immediately, with Baylor as president and Tryon as either corresponding secretary or vice president. The object of the body was "To assist in procuring an education for those young men who give evidence of being called of God to preach the Gospel, and who shall have the approbation of their respective churches."[8] Any person was eligible to become a member of the society, regardless of denominational affiliation, but members of the executive committee were required to be Baptists.

The creation of a society of this nature to promote Baptist educational interests was not original with Texas Baptists. It had been a well-tested method within the denomination for at least twenty-five years. Following the religious awakening of the early 1800s, Baptists had sought ways to spread the Gospel across the world. Missionary societies were quickly organized for this purpose. In 1814 most of these societies united to form the General Missionary Convention of the Baptist Denomination in the United States of America for Foreign Missions. At the second session of that body, which met only every third year, the delegates seriously began considering ways to improve the educational level of the ministry. The result of that concern was the formation of education societies across the denomination.[9]

The growth of both the missionary and the education societies during the next two decades was phenomenal, as almost every state in the Union established at least one such organization. Originally created to provide financial support to ministerial students, the education societies actually became catalysts for the creation of institutions in which aspiring preachers could train. Most of the schools established by such societies had both a literary and a theological orientation. However, the number of students pursuing a ministerial education was usually much lower than those enrolled for a general education.

By the early 1830s, Baptist preparatory and collegiate institutions had spread from New England to Georgia. In most of the schools, students paid their tuition and fees from whatever resources were available to them. In others, such as Mercer Institute, which Tryon attended, the manual labor principle — uniting work and study — was followed. In the majority of schools of that kind, the work of the students helped finance the institution's operation and contributed to lower operating costs. By 1841, Baptists across the United States boasted more than a dozen colleges, as well as numerous preparatory institutions.

The original reason for the formation of education societies across the United States was to enhance educational opportunities for ministerial students. The method chosen to provide this education had been the creation of institutions of learning. Such was the hope of Tryon, who had personally benefited from Baptist funding of his education. James Huckins, who was named to the original board of managers of the Texas Baptist Education Society, was another who had received Baptist support, when he had attended Brown University in Providence, Rhode Island. He, like most of the other members of the society, recognized the value of a Baptist university in Texas, and was desirous of seeing one established.

Unfortunately, all plans for such an endeavor had to be postponed because of the invasions of Generals Vasquez and Woll in 1842. Only informal meetings of the Education Society were held that year and the next. It was not until the society was reorganized in 1844 that it was able to return to its original objective. Among those elected to lead the rejuvenated body were R. E. B. Baylor as president and William Tryon as vice president.[10]

One of the first orders of business was the decision to seek from the Texas Congress a charter for an institution upon a plan "so broad that the requirements of existing conditions would be fully met."[11] The "existing conditions" referred to the need for educating ministers, as well as those interested only in secular learning. In addition to meeting the immediate needs, the society wanted to establish an institution that "would be fully susceptible of enlargement and development to meet the demand of all ages to come."[12] To petition Congress for the charter, the group selected Baylor, Tryon, and J. G. Thomas, corresponding secretary of the society.

Thomas was a trained lawyer and a leader in the Baptist church in Caldwell, where Tryon had often preached since its constitution in May 1843. Only recently elected as clerk of the Union Association, Thomas was contemplating becoming a minister.[13] The precise part he played either in the development of the petition or in assisting its passage through both houses of Congress is not known, but he probably had only a very minor role.

Shortly after the fall 1844 meeting of the society, Baylor visited Tryon at his farm at Hildalgo Bluff. There he dictated the words of the required petition to Tryon, who recorded them on paper. One of the items in the request to Congress stipulated that no money or land was desired or would be accepted from the government. Even though other denominations had requested and received donations from the Congress, Baylor and Tryon considered this against their principles. At a later date Baylor wrote to James Huckins and explained the reasoning behind this section of the petition. He stated that both he and Tryon felt that by asking for money from the government the request would have had a tendency to encourage the government to give preference to one religious sect against another, as the lawmakers could decide to give to one group and not another. In his letter he added that he was thankful that "we have gone on relying upon his [God] blessings and the private charity of noble and generous friends, and [as a result] we may say with truth that our university ranks among the first in the state."[14]

No decision was made on this occasion about a name for the institution. Thus, when it was presented on the Senate floor on 28 December 1844, it was simply presented as "the petition of R. E. B. Baylor, and others, praying the incorporation of a College or University, for the purpose of a more general diffusion of useful knowledge."[15] Two days later, when the bill was read for the second time, the name San Jacinto University was added.[16]

It was then sent to the committee on the State of the Republic for review. This committee reported it back to the Senate on 3 January 1845 recommending passage.[17] On the following day it was presented for another reading, after which it was laid on the table.[18] It was taken up again on 7 January, and a motion was passed to strike out San Jacinto wherever it occurred in the bill and to insert Milam.[19] The bill, now entitled "an act to incorporate the Milam University" came up for the third and final reading on 8 January. On this occasion, Senator George A. Patillo, the original sponsor of the bill and the one who had suggested changing the name from San Jacinto to Milam, sought yet another revision. This one replaced the name of Milam with that of Baylor.[20] This change was approved by the Senate chamber and was then forwarded to the House for its consideration.

The name of Baylor evidently had been selected during the ten days of deliberations in the upper house. R. E. B. Baylor felt that the name Tryon would be the most appropriate choice, since the original idea of founding a university had been his, and because Tryon had worked so hard toward its accomplishment. Tryon, however, felt that some might misunderstand the motives of his labors, and refused to allow his name to be considered. Instead, he suggested that the institution should be named for Baylor, who also demurred for similar reasons, as well as because he claimed to feel unworthy of such a distinction. However, Tryon and Kenneth Anderson, President of the Senate and newly inaugurated Vice President of the Republic, were determined, and eventually Baylor acquiesced.[21]

On 9 January, the bill to incorporate Baylor University was read in the House for the first time.[22] Twelve days later it was considered again, and then was sent to a select committee. This group quickly reviewed it, and later that day recommended passage.[23] The bill received its third reading on 25 January, after which it was approved.[24] The charter was then signed by Anderson in his official capacity as President of the Senate, and by John M. Lewis, Speaker of the House. Texas President Anson Jones affixed his signature on 1 February, just three days before the adjournment of the Ninth, and final, Congress of the

Republic.

The charter authorized fifteen trustees, almost all of whom were prominent Baptists, to operate the university. The first meeting of this body was set for 7 April 1845 at Independence. When a quorum failed to arrive, the meeting was rescheduled for Brenham on 15 May. Tryon did not attend either of these sessions, since he was in the United States, where he had gone earlier in the spring to escape the heat of the Texas summer and to acquire books for the Baptist book depository that he was attempting to establish at Washington-on-the-Brazos.

Because of inadequate printing facilities in the republic, only a few publications other than newspapers were being printed there, none of which was of a religious nature. Most educational materials were published in the northern United States. Assuming that many people had acquired through the years more than an adequate supply of religious periodicals and books, Tryon, while in New York in July, made a special appeal for donations in the *New York Recorder.* He requested the readers of the newspaper to donate a few volumes from their personal libraries to the people in Texas who, he explained, were in dire need of religious reading material.[25] There is no evidence to indicate whether his plea was heeded or ignored.

Tryon returned to Texas sometime in the fall of 1845. Shortly thereafter, he learned of the actions of the trustees during his absence. They had selected Independence as the site for the new school and had named him to the building committee. They also had unanimously elected him as president of the university's board.[26]

In December Tryon attended his first trustee meeting, during which he resigned from the building committee. He considered the work of this committee very important, especially since the institution as yet had no facilities in which to conduct classes. But, having just accepted the pastorate of the Baptist church in Houston, he felt that his physical separation from the planned campus would prohibit his active involvement in any building endeavors.

He did not relinquish any other responsibilities, however. During the second week of January 1846, he journeyed from

Houston to Independence to participate in a called meeting, even though he had just moved to his new church field. The major items on the agenda were the selection of the first president and the first teacher of the preparatory school.

For the presidency the trustees chose thirty-three-year-old Henry L. Graves.[27] A Baptist minister, Graves was an 1833 honor graduate of the University of North Carolina and had taught at Wake Forest College. He had attended the Hamilton Literary and Theological Institute at Hamilton, New York, from 1840 to 1842, and since that time had been teaching at Covington, Georgia.[28]

Following the selection of Graves, the board then elected Henry F. Gillett, an Episcopalian, to head the preparatory department. Gillett had been in Texas for six years, during which time he had taught school in Houston and in Washington County. While teaching at Union Academy near Washington-on-the-Brazos from 1841 to 1843, he had boarded with James Farquhar, a charter Baylor trustee and deacon of the Washington Baptist Church. Tryon had officiated at Gillett's wedding in March 1842.[29]

In other actions the trustees named Tryon, R. E. B. Baylor, and Hosea Garrett to the bylaws committee. The original committee had been appointed at the May 1845 meeting, but thus far had been unable to develop the necessary articles for the board's consideration. Although not a trustee, Garrett had attended the previous meetings of the body as proxy for absent trustees. At this session he was serving as proxy for A. G. Haynes. The placement of these men on the committee apparently brought about the desired results, as the bylaws were quickly completed and approved.

Also at this meeting, the trustees decided to build a permanent structure in which to conduct collegiate studies, and to repair the former Independence Academy building for use by the preparatory school.[30] The latter structure may have been the same one used by Miss Frances Trask, a twenty-eight-year-old lady from Massachusetts who had started the first girls' school in Texas in 1834.[31] Her school had ceased to operate during the revolution in 1836, and about a year later, Congress chartered the

Independence Academy. That institution may also have held classes in the facilities formerly occupied by Miss Trask.[32] Some time after the academy's close in 1845, E. W. Taylor, one of the trustees named in the charter of Baylor University, purchased the building at a sheriff's auction. When the Baylor board was deciding among the bids of Huntsville, Travis, Shannon's Prairie, and Independence for location of the school, the availability of this property had tipped the scales in favor of Independence.[33]

Within a week after returning to Houston from the Baylor trustee meeting, Tryon became engaged in another educational matter. This one was nondenominational, and had the potential of affecting school-aged children throughout Texas. At the end of December 1845, the Republic of Texas had been annexed to the United States. Though some loose ends still remained, Texas was technically the twenty-eighth state of the Union. Because of this, many religious and secular educational leaders felt a pressing need to establish a uniform, state-wide system of education.

It was for this purpose that Tryon and other friends of education gathered in Houston in the third week of January 1846 to form the Texas Literary Institute. Tryon's interest in education and his reputation as a leader in the field were widely known. As a result, he was elected treasurer of the group. The Reverend Chauncey Richardson, head of Rutersville College, was chosen president. R. E. B. Baylor was named to a three-man committee charged with creating greater interest in education throughout Texas.[34]

Among the goals of the Texas Literary Institute were the establishment of a program of public instruction adapted to the needs of Texas; the creation of male and female academies, common or district schools, and one or more colleges and universities; and the development of a systematic mode of instruction.[35]

Though supportive of the institute's plans, Tryon had little time to spend in its behalf before he left a few weeks later for the east coast of the United States. Several denominations in Houston had permanent church buildings in which to conduct worship services. Tryon's congregation had no such facilities, however, and had to meet in homes or in rented rooms. Recognizing the importance of a permanent worship center, and realizing that little money was available among the Baptists in Houston for such a purpose, Tryon had personally felt compelled to solicit funds from the Baptists in the more established states. Therefore, he spent the next several months traveling across the South and the East, seeking money with which to pay for the construction of a new church building.

In late May, when he returned to Houston, he brought back several hundred dollars in cash and much more in subscriptions. He also carried a commission from the Board of Domestic Missions of the Southern Baptist Convention. Originally appointed to Texas by the American Baptist Home Mission Society in 1840, Tryon had been reappointed by that body annually since then. His last renewal had been in January 1845. However, for unknown reasons he had not requested consideration for reemployment by the Home Mission Society for 1846.

During Tryon's travels in the older states on behalf of the Houston church, James Huckins, pastor of the Galveston church, was also on a similar mission for his congregation. It was because of Huckins that Tryon had been named a Southern Baptist missionary.

In March 1846, Huckins had met with the executive committee of the Georgia Baptist Convention to seek its endorsement of his efforts. Not only did the committee endorse him, but it also wrote to the Board of Domestic Missions and recommended that both he and Tryon be appointed missionaries of the Southern Baptist Convention. The executive committee assured the inadequately financed mission board that sufficient money for the salaries of Huckins and Tryon would be forthcoming from Georgia Baptists.[36] As a result, Huckins and Tryon, along with four others who were assigned to various states, became the first missionary appointees of the Southern Baptist Convention.

Shortly after Tryon's return, the Houston congregation approved contracts for its two-thousand-square-foot brick worship center. The building was to contain a large auditorium, a vestry, a gallery for singers, and a baptistry under the pulpit. Cost for the facility was estimated to be about four thousand dollars.[37]

As the building began to take shape, the Houston congregation was seemingly imbued with renewed spiritual vigor. Though still small in number, the congregation decided to organize a Sunday school to help meet the religious educational needs of the community. To do so, they formed the Houston Baptist Sunday School Society and made it auxiliary to the American Sunday School Union.[38]

Established in 1824, the American Sunday School Union was an outgrowth of the Sunday school movement which had begun in the United States in the mid-1700s. Since its organization the Union had grown to become the major Sunday school promotional group in America. However, no special efforts had been made by that body in Texas until early in 1846, when the annexation of the republic had been assured.

Sunday schools had existed in Texas since 1829, when Thomas J. Pilgrim established the first one at San Felipe de Austin. It did not last long, for he soon abandoned it out of fear of the Mexican government, which prohibited all religious teaching other than Catholicism. Following the independence of Texas, Sunday schools sprang up throughout the country. Some of these Sunday schools were denominationally oriented, but most were community-based.

Even though there already were three Sunday schools operating in Houston, Tryon and his congregation felt that the needs of the four thousand residents of the city were great enough to justify the foundation of a fourth. Thus, on 6 July the members of the First Baptist Church gathered at the old city hall and established their own Sunday school.

James Burke, agent of the American Sunday School Union, was the main speaker for the organizational ceremonies. He was deeply impressed with the determination of this small group of Baptists. As was his custom, he offered to make a gift of several books for the church's library. Tryon refused to accept them at no charge. He preferred instead to stretch the scant financial resources within the membership and pay for the literature.[39] Though a small gesture, it was perhaps indicative of Tryon's faith in the future of the Houston congregation.

5

BY THE FALL OF 1846, William Tryon's faith in the small group of people who had called him as their pastor the previous December had been justified. The church membership had grown to thirty-four, an increase of more than 300 percent; the new Sunday school had eight teachers, sixty children were enrolled, and numerous adults were attending weekly Bible classes.[1]

Since his commission as a Southern Baptist missionary in the spring, the pace that Tryon had set in sharing the Gospel had been phenomenal. He had preached seventy-two sermons, delivered ninety lectures, and attended at least two religious meetings a week, apart from those at which he spoke. In addition, he had made 250 visits to the members of his church and to others in Houston to whom he ministered.

Even though he was extremely busy with the various activities of his church, the Texas Literary Institute, and Baylor University, Tryon did not neglect his leadership responsibilities with the Union Baptist Association. This body had been organized in October 1840, only three months before Tryon arrived in Texas. The few men who established it had represented only three churches with a combined membership of forty-five. Although there were a few other congregations in what was then known as "western" Texas, they had not sent delegates to the organizational meeting, which had been held at Travis. Thomas W. Cox was pastor of the three churches represented, and he naturally was elected moderator of the newly formed association. R. E. B. Baylor was chosen as the organization's corresponding secretary.

Cox, Baylor, and Tryon frequently conducted protracted meetings together in the spring and summer of 1841. During this period, Cox had minor confrontations with both Tryon and Baylor because of his promotion of the doctrines of Alexander Campbell, especially the principles that dictated that baptism was essential for salvation. The first major clash did not occur, however, until the first anniversary meeting of the Union Baptist Association in early October.

For this meeting delegates gathered at the Clear Creek church near La Grange. One of the sermons preached during the meeting was by Cox, who as pastor of the church followed it with an invitation for those who wished to present themselves for membership. Tryon and several others felt that the sermon clearly advocated the principles of Campbellism. In response they requested that the proposed new members voice their Christian experience.[2] Such a controversy arose over the propriety of that demand that a postponement was declared in accepting the new members.[3] When the association adjourned, Tryon, who had been elected moderator, and a few other ministers requested that Z. N. Morrell stay at La Grange to present appropriate charges of heresy against Cox at the next business conference of the Clear Creek church. Though he had other pressing responsibilities, Morrell accepted because he felt obligated to pursue the matter. A few days later, he presented the heresy charges, as well as information about alleged fraud stemming from Cox's activities during his Alabama pastorate two years earlier. Those complaints were reviewed and resulted in heated debate among the church members. When the arguments from both sides concluded, a vote was taken, and Cox and his followers were excluded from the church.[4]

Though removed from the leadership of the Clear Creek church, Cox still pastored the Travis church and shared the pulpit with Tryon at Independence, where the congregation was divided between support and disavowal of Cox's Campbellite teachings. Within the Independence community was a married couple who had recently arrived from the South. The man had been an active deacon in a Baptist church prior to moving to Texas, but both he and his wife hesitated to join the Independence congregation because of the divergent theological views being espoused there, and because of fear of involvement in an intradenominational feud.

Their attitude changed dramatically one Sunday, after they had heard a sermon in which Tryon graphically illustrated the obligations and responsibilities of all true followers of Christ. Deeply impressed, the couple offered themselves and were accepted for membership. As anticipated, controversy soon arose over the views of Cox. When a vote was called to determine whether Tryon or Cox should become the church's sole pastor, the man and his wife sided with Tryon's followers, making the vote fourteen to thirteen in favor of removing Cox from the pulpit.[5]

The situation was similar at Travis, the other church pastored by Cox. There, however, a majority of the congregation favored the Campbellite principles, and voted to exclude all those opposed. As a result, Cox remained at the helm of that church even though he had been discredited by two others. By mid-1842, however, Cox had resigned the Travis church pulpit, and Tryon and Baylor became co-pastors of the congregation.[6]

Except for the disturbances engendered by the controversies concerning Cox, the Baptists of "western" Texas experienced a prosperous first year as an association. Nine churches became active in the work of this body, the four largest of which were pastored by Tryon. Of the approximately two hundred people reported baptized between October 1840 and September 1841, all but about twenty-five were influenced to some degree by the preaching of Tryon, who at this time had been in Texas for only some eight months.

The Mexican invasions of 1842 greatly disturbed many Baptist activities in Texas, and drastically slowed the growth of the denomination. Even so, when the delegates assembled for the associational meeting at Mt. Gilead Baptist Church in November, interest in spreading the Gospel was paramount among their objectives. To lead them in this path, the representatives reelected Tryon as moderator and Baylor as corresponding secretary. They also invited Tryon to preach the associational sermon and named him to the committee to revise the constitution, bylaws, and rules of decorum. In addition, Tryon was placed on the editorial, book, and executive committees.

The number of responsibilities given him in the affairs of the association was matched by the workload he shouldered in his day-to-day activities. The total membership of the churches in the association was 433. Tryon, as pastor of the Providence, Washington, Mt. Gilead, and Independence churches, was the spiritual shepherd of almost 60 percent of them.

Ministering to this number of people was taxing, but Tryon enjoyed the challenge, especially when the results justified his efforts. Although the number of those joining the Baptist faith during 1842 was much smaller than in the previous year, still Tryon had the privilege of baptizing almost half of the forty-two who were converted.

The following year, at the October 1843 associational conference, the delegates recognized his successful leadership efforts and reelected him moderator. They also placed upon him the additional responsibility of establishing a religious book depository at Washington-on-the-Brazos.[7] At this meeting, the members of the association instituted a program of regional conferences to be held the following year in addition to the annual meeting. The purpose of these sessions was to stimulate interest and support of various associational activities. Tryon, of course, was expected to participate in as many of these as possible.

During 1844, several Baptist preachers moved into Texas. As a result, Tryon was able to decrease the number of his trips across the republic to share the Gospel. He continued, however, to pastor the Independence, Washington, and Mt. Gilead churches. These three congregations comprised more than half the total membership in the sixteen-church association.[8] Throughout the year, Tryon's denominational leadership continued to be appreciated. When the Union Baptist Association met for its fifth anniversary in August, Tryon was once again chosen as its moderator. It was the fourth time in as many sessions that he had received this recognition.

Taking advantage of his position as moderator, Tryon attempted to establish more consistent administrative and organizational procedures within the association. He worked closely with the committee charged with responsibility for drafting rules for constituting churches, and he assisted another group in making changes in the articles of faith.[9] He also used the association's circular letter to suggest specific principles of operation.

Because of the distances between the Baptist congregations, and the resulting inadequate communication, circular letters often were used to inform the total membership of the association about various plans and activities. The letters also were mailed to religious groups in other parts of Texas and the United States to share information.

In the 1844 circular letter, Tryon broached the subject of administrative procedures involved in the disciplining and the reception of church members. His theme was that both should be handled carefully and with love. In the epistle he also discussed the role that Christians should play in improving the quality of life in Texas. He wrote

> The Bible tells us that the Church is the light of the world; but if the light that is in this new country be darkness, how great is that darkness! Society, in Texas, is far from being thoroughly organized — executive, legislative and judicial power exert but a feeble influence over this tumultuous sea of passion; it is for the Church to pour oil upon the troubled waves! It is for the followers of Christ to disseminate the examples of forbearance, and to discountenance those broils and

> feuds which set law and government at defiance, and are the blast and mildew of our country.[10]

His opinion was that the followers of Christ had a unique obligation to set the example for all of society's activities.

In addition to his associational responsibilities, Tryon was active in the work of the Texas Home Mission Society. That body had been created as a separate entity by the Union Baptist Association in October 1841. At its inaugural meeting, held during a recess of the associational gathering, five hundred dollars was subscribed. This money was used to employ A. A. Buffington as the first missionary of the society. The organization was officially recognized as an auxiliary of the American Baptist Home Mission Society in July 1842. James Huckins was president during its first three years. In 1844 and 1845 Tryon served as the corresponding secretary.[11]

When the association met in October 1845, Tryon did not participate because he was still in the United States soliciting support for the establishment of the association's book depository. Because of his absence, he was not elected moderator. He was not forgotten, however, for the delegates chose him to deliver the associational sermon the following year. As a part of the sermon, they suggested that Tryon set forth the principles and history of the Baptist denomination.[12] He probably was one of only a few men in Texas who could adequately handle this assignment.

When the Union Association met at Caldwell in October 1846, Tryon was present and ready. His sermon was a miniature portrait of the history of the Baptist denomination from the days of Jesus Christ to the present. Citing numerous authorities and Scriptures, Tryon's message attested to the validity and purpose of the Baptist faith, and concluded with a plea for "the Lord in his infinite mercy [to] hasten the time when Christians shall all see eye to eye, and pull together like horses in Pharaoh's chariot."[13] This was, perhaps, one of Tryon's deepest desires.

James Huckins was so impressed with Tryon's message that he recommended it be published and distributed in lieu of the normal circular letter. His suggestion was heartily approved by the other delegates.[14]

6

AS DECEMBER 1846 DREW to a close, William Tryon could reflect with exultant satisfaction upon his work with the Houston Baptist Church, Baylor University, Texas Literary Institute, and the Union Baptist Association. Each was experiencing unprecedented success, and prospects for the future seemed even more bountiful.

The Houston church was growing in numbers and spirit. Construction of the worship center was well under way, and the Sunday school was continually attracting new members. Interest and support of the Texas Literary Institute was rapidly increasing across the state. At Baylor, the renovation of the old Independence Academy building was nearly complete, and seventy students were enrolled for the second semester. Membership in the Union Association had reached twenty churches, several of which were newly constituted congregations.

In addition, three recently appointed Southern Baptist missionaries had arrived to strengthen the ranks of the ministry in the state. Though the war between the United States and

Mexico, which had been declared in the spring, was of grave concern to the people of Texas and the United States, the resultant patriotic fervor and news reports of American victories were spurring a mild prosperity across the land.

Tryon's family, which now numbered five, included his wife and three children — William Armistead, four; Ella Louise, three; and Ann Baylor, almost two years old. He owned a house and a lot in Houston, several slaves, almost four thousand acres in surrounding counties, and a ten-acre tract on the Buffalo Bayou.

In spite of the level of achievement that Tryon was experiencing, he was not completely happy. He had begun to have premonitions that his life was approaching its end.[1] Though he never expressed the thought that 1847 might be his last year, it soon became obvious that he wanted to do more with his life during whatever time might remain to him.

He manifested this desire through increased zeal in his work and greater involvement in other areas of interest. One such arena of endeavor involved female education. Feeling that educational opportunities for young ladies in Houston were limited, Tryon began to champion a campaign to establish a new school for girls in the town. The result of his efforts was the creation by mid-1847 of the Houston Female Institute. Tryon, of course, was named as one of its founding trustees.[2]

Tryon's new zest for life was emulated by many within his church, and he reported in *The Southern Baptist Missionary Journal* that "There are indications of seriousness in our congregation, which are quite encouraging."[3] This indirectly resulted in a greater interest among the members in raising funds to hasten the completion of the church's worship center. The Houston congregation's activities were observed and soon followed by citizens of Lynchburg. In this small community about a day's ride south from Houston, many of the townsfolk felt the need for a worship center and decided to construct one that could be shared by several faiths. Tryon and James Huckins were requested to occupy the pulpit on the Sundays designated for the Baptist denomination.[4]

In February 1847, the Texas Literary Institute began

publication of a small pamphlet, with the intent of issuing it monthly. Entitled "The Public School Advocate," its purposes were to inform the public of the plight of education in the state and to garner support from various quarters for the development of common schools.[5] Annual subscription fees of one dollar were necessary to defray the printing expenses. Tryon, as the recently reelected treasurer of the Institute, was vital to this drive.

In addition to soliciting subscriptions for the Literary Institute, Tryon also had a fund-raising responsibility on behalf of Baylor University. In February 1846, the trustees of the institution had requested several individuals to serve voluntarily as financial agents for the school.[6] Among those asked to seek donations were Tryon, president-elect Henry L. Graves, and the Reverend Rufus C. Burleson, a student of the Western Baptist Theological Seminary in Covington, Kentucky. Burleson had been assigned an area that included Ohio, Mississippi, and Alabama. As compensation for his work, he was allowed to keep 10 percent of all monies he collected.[7]

Burleson was known to have an interest in serving Christ in Texas, and had previously been contacted by Tryon in an effort to persuade him to make that commitment.[8] He was only one of many preachers whom Tryon had attempted to persuade during the past few years to journey to Texas. Some of those whom he had encouraged were already in the Lone Star State. A few others were still considering a move westward.[9]

Just as Tryon was convinced that Texas was the most promising field of labor for Baptist ministers, he also felt certain that Baylor University offered the greatest hope for the denomination's future in the state. In a letter printed in the September 1847 issue of *The Southern Baptist Missionary Journal* Tryon stated that

> I consider our Literary Institution calculated, with God's blessing, to do more towards securing permanency to our denomination than any other movement with which I have been connected since my removal from Alabama. It is a nucleus around which the denomination will rally; and will become a school

> of the Prophets, from which, in years to come, their children will go forth as missionaries to various parts of the world.[10]

During the spring of 1847, however, prospects for the future of the university did not appear quite so hopeful. Sickness and bad weather had caused many of the seventy who had entered the preparatory department's second semester to leave school. The curtailed enrollment drastically reduced the amount of income from what had originally been anticipated by the trustees. Similar shortfalls had been among the major causes of failure in many of the earlier schools in Texas, and some persons connected with Baylor sensed impending disaster. In spite of predictions of possible failure, Tryon remained optimistic about the university's future. Its advantages of location, climate, and potential denominational support convinced him that the lull in the cash flow would prove to be only temporary. His positive attitude may have played a part in his unanimous reelection to the presidency of the board of trustees during the last week in April.[11]

As Tryon began another year of service for Baylor, he concluded his first year's appointment as a missionary of the Southern Baptist Convention. Since his appointment in the spring of 1846, he had preached 156 sermons, had delivered 154 lectures on religious subjects, had attended 70 prayer meetings and 65 other religious meetings, and had made 440 pastoral visits.

May 1847 also was a special milestone in the life of the Houston Baptist Church. In the past year, more than thirty-five new members had joined, the Sunday school had increased to seventy students, and the library now contained more than 150 volumes. The church building was complete, and Tryon often had heard people speak of it as the best piece of masonry in the state.[12] Its eighteen-inch-thick walls testified to its soundness. At the dedication of the facility on the last Sunday in May, a large crowd of members and visitors participated in ceremonies led by Tryon, Baylor president Henry L. Graves, and Galveston Baptist Church pastor James Huckins.[13]

A few weeks later, the Houston congregation decided to enhance further the new building and contracted for the installation of stained glass windows.[14] They also sought to enhance Tryon's financial status by pledging to him all funds raised from the renting of the pews for the next twelve months. The number of pews is unknown, but the minimum annual rental price was fifteen dollars each.[15]

Later that summer, the Galveston Baptist Church congregation completed its year-long sanctuary building program. Unfortunately, Huckins, who had almost single-handedly raised the necessary funds for the construction of the facility, was too sick to participate in the dedication ceremonies, which were held in the second week of September. Because of Huckins's illness, Tryon was called upon to lead the services, in which several ministers from other denominations in the island city also participated.[16]

Following the dedication of the Galveston church, Tryon returned to Houston to make the necessary preparations for the anniversary meeting of the Union Baptist Association, which was scheduled to be held in his church later that month.

It had been a good year for the association. Since October 1846, 265 people had joined its various congregations — only about 70 less than the total number who had joined the churches of this body in all the years since 1841. Among them all, the Houston church led in number of additions, with 23 joining by baptism and 11 by letter. Its total membership now stood at 69, an increase of 62 during Tryon's pastorate of some twenty months.

During the meeting of the association, the delegates chose Tryon to serve once again as moderator. He was also requested to deliver the 1848 introductory sermon, and to serve as alternate preacher for the associational sermon. This was the fifth time Tryon had been invited to speak before this body, but it was the first and only occasion any individual had ever been named to give one of the conference's major addresses, and to serve also as alternate for the other. Evidently, Tryon's pulpit oratory was so much appreciated that the delegates wanted to make certain they would hear him at least once. The odds of their hearing him twice were good, as the alternate often replaced the designated speaker, who frequently failed to attend associational functions because of other responsibilities, sickness, or transportation problems.

The report of the association's growth was impressive to its delegates. To ensure similar future expansion in the denomination, most of those present recognized a need for improvement in communication among congregations. The method selected to achieve this objective was to form new, more closely clustered associations of churches that relied upon each other for administrative functions and support. Consequently, five churches, all located in or near Lavaca County, were authorized to form their own association. Tryon and five others were selected to assist in the constitution of this new body in November.[17]

On Saturday, the third day of the meeting, the association suspended its afternoon activities to permit those interested in the Texas Baptist Education Society to participate in that body's annual conference. At this session, the society's appreciation for Tryon's leadership was manifested again, as the membership elected him their president — a fitting tribute for the individual whose idea in 1841 had led to the creation of the society.[18]

When the association reconvened on Monday morning, a project which Tryon recently had been promoting — the combination of all Baptist churches in Texas into a single state-wide convention — took a first step toward fruition. A Central Committee of Correspondence was named to assist Henry L. Graves, the association's corresponding secretary, in determining the degree of interest of the various congregations throughout Texas in the formation of such an organization. Tryon was among the nine men chosen to direct this endeavor.[19]

A general spirit of optimism permeated all sessions of the association, and when Tryon composed its circular letter, he seemed to capture this mood and the delegates' eager anticipation of the future. One of the areas about which the members of the association were hopeful related to renewed financial support for ministers. Because so many of the Baptist churches in Texas were small, pastors often had to seek other employment in addition to the income received from their pastoral assignments. Tryon believed, as did most others in the association, that the time had arrived for preachers and their congregations to launch out on faith in service to Christ. Because of this conviction, Tryon used the circular letter to exhort the various congregations to make a special effort to become the sole support of their pastors. He also encouraged the pastors to seek additional education, in order to serve the members of their churches more effectively. The conclusion was an emphatic promise that

> a better state of things has dawned upon our country! The Lone Star is now clustered in the galaxy which represents the Free States of the North American Union!
>
> The tide of emigration is now pouring into our lovely country, and from this emigration our churches are receiving most valuable acquisitions. The Lord has blessed us! The armies of locusts and caterpillars have not marched through our land! Our fields have produced abundantly, so that we have scarcely room where to bestow our fruits and goods.
>
> Brethren, we feel assured that you will take into consideration the subject we have placed before you. That you will say to your Preachers, leave your School Houses! Leave your Farms! Give yourselves to study! Give yourselves wholly to the Ministry of the Word. You shall suffer no loss. Your families shall be sustained.[20]

The enthusiasm for the Lord's work which was so prevalent during all the sessions of the association sparked an evangelistic hunger among the delegates. Therefore, when the time came for adjournment, most were not ready to leave. Instead, they called for Tryon and several other ministers to lead a series of worship services. For the next two weeks, the sanctuary of the Houston church was filled with large audiences who gathered to hear the principles of Christianity extolled. During this protracted meeting, Tryon baptized nineteen people and received four into the membership of his church by letter. In addition to the public decisions recorded, Tryon was convinced that there were many others in the congregation who felt a deep concern for the salvation of their souls.[21]

Immediately following the close of these services, Tryon turned his attention to the affairs of the Houston Female Institute, which had begun its first term on 20 September in a small building in the southwestern part of the city.[22] As a trustee of the school, Tryon's principal interest was in its proper organization and administration. The institution seemed to have general support from the community, but there was little evidence at this time to indicate whether it would prove a success or a failure.

About six weeks later, the Texas Literary Institute met in Houston for its annual conference. The morning session was primarily devoted to business and to the election of officers, most of whom were reelected, including Tryon as treasurer. James Burke, Tryon's close friend and agent of the American Sunday School Union, was chosen corresponding secretary. As corresponding secretary, Burke became the leading advocate in the organization's decision to request five hundred dollars from the legislature to fund the society's publication, the "Public School Advocate." Though that probably was a legitimate and honorable cause upon which to expend tax revenues, no funds were ever granted to the institute by the state for this purpose.

In other business during the day, those present decided not to seek from legislators the immediate establishment of a specific system of education for the entire state, even though that was the major objective of the organization. Evidently they felt that such an attempt would not prove expedient, because public sentiment had not yet been sufficiently aroused to lead to a favorable decision.[23]

At the evening convocation, held in the Houston Baptist Church, Tryon was among the featured speakers. He was heard by a large audience, who seemed greatly interested in the future development of education.[24]

Though the one-day conference was well attended, there probably were scores with similar interests across the state who did not participate because of reports in various newspapers of an outbreak of yellow fever in Houston. Many persons in the interior of Texas refrained from traveling to any coastal area during the summer and fall because of dread of this little understood and often fatal disease. Because of past epidemics in and around Houston, quite a few inhabitants of low-lying communities annually vacated their residences in early fall, and journeyed north for safety. Tryon had been advised to leave and live temporarily on his property in Washington County, but he had felt that his responsibilities to his church members and to others in the city who might need him far outweighed the risk of danger to himself. In fact, during the two months preceding the gathering in Houston of the friends of education, Tryon had ministered to many in the city who were sick with the fever. One of these was Tryon's close friend, Isaac Van Zandt, who had been stricken by the disease in early October while campaigning for the governorship. Most people acknowledged Van Zandt to be the front runner for the office, but yellow fever proved not to be a respecter of persons.

During Van Zandt's illness, Tryon had visited him frequently, and when he died on 11 October, his funeral was held in the Houston Baptist Church. Though he had never united with a church in Texas, while on his death bed he confessed to Tryon his personal faith in Christ. At his burial, Tryon eulogized Van Zandt as a great statesman and a leader of men, and claimed that his death was a unique loss to Texas, especially in the political arena.[25]

Less than a month later, only a few days after participating in the meeting of the Texas Literary Institute, Tryon himself contracted yellow fever. After struggling with the debilitating disease for ten days, he finally succumbed on 16 November 1847. He was only thirty-eight years old, and some felt he was in the height of his usefulness in God's work.[26] His death was certainly a heavy blow to his family, friends and colleagues, and the sudden removal of his leadership in Texas educational and religious circles was deeply felt by many, who mourned him across the country.

Though gone after so brief a sojourn, his work was to endure, for during his almost seven years in Texas he had been a most effective pastor, educator, evangelist, counselor — and, as R. E. B. Baylor said, the embodiment and form of religion. As a servant of Christ, William Milton Tryon had been, indeed, a noble example.

Notes

Chapter 1

1. R. E. B. Baylor to James Huckins, 1 March 1859. Original in the R. E. B. Baylor Papers, The Texas Collection, Baylor University, Waco, Texas.

2. J. B. Link, ed., *Texas Historical and Biographical Magazine,* vol. 1 (Austin: 1891), 170.

3. Z. N. Morrell, *Flowers and Fruits from the Wilderness; or, Thirty-Six Years and Two Winters in Honduras* (1872; reprint, Waco, Tex.: The Markham Press Fund of Baylor University Press, 1976), 135.

4. R. E. B. Baylor to James Huckins, 1 March 1859.

5. "Galveston Baptist Church, Minutes," 30 January 1840, photocopy at the Rosenberg Library, Galveston.

6. *The Southern Baptist Missionary Journal,* May 1849, 283.

7. B. H. Carroll, ed., *Standard History of Houston, Texas* (Knoxville, Tenn.: H. W. Crew & Co., 1912), 143.

8. Link, *Texas Hist. and Bio. Magazine,* 1:369.

9. "Records of the First Baptist Church in Houston," 1 December 1845, photocopy at The Southwestern Baptist Theological Seminary, Fort Worth, Texas.

10. Wes M. Tryon, ed., *The Tryon Family in America* (Wheaton, Md., 1969), n.p.

11. Ibid.

12. Billington McCarter Sanders, "The History of Mercer University, 1829-1850," *The Christian Index,* 25 December 1920.

13. Ibid.

14. Rufus Washington Weaver, "The History of Mercer University," *The Christian Index,* 25 December 1920.

15. Untitled article in *The Christian Index,* date unknown, archives, Mercer University, Macon, Georgia.

16. Ibid.

17. Ibid.

18. Billington M. Sanders to Samuel Wait, 15 October 1833, typescript in Mercer History file, archives, Mercer University.

19. "Mercer Institute, Account Book, 1833-1835," archives, Mercer University.

20. Spright Dowell, *A History of Mercer University,* 1833-1953 (Macon, Georgia: Mercer University, 1958), 141.

21. *Minutes of the 14th Anniversary of the Georgia Baptist Convention, Held at Shiloh, Green County, 22-25 May, 1835* (Washington, Ga.: Office of *The Christian Index,* 1835), 7.

22. *Minutes of the 15th Anniversary of the Georgia Baptist Convention, Held at Talbottom, Ga., 29-30 April and 2-3 May, 1836* (Washington: *Christian Index,* 1836), 8; "Minutes, Executive Committee, Georgia Baptist Convention," 2 March 1836, archives, Mercer University.

23. *History of the Baptist Denomination in Georgia: With Biographical Compendium and Portrait Gallery of Baptist Ministers and other Georgia Baptists* (Atlanta: Compiled for *The Christian Index,* J. P. Harrison & Co., 1881), 186.

24. *Minutes of the Sixteenth Anniversary of the Georgia Baptist Convention, Held at Ruckersville, Georgia on the 5th, 6th and 8th of May, 1837* (Washington, Ga.: *The Christian Index* Office, 1837), 10.

25. Ibid., 8.

26. "Minutes, Executive Committee," 6 May 1837.

27. Eugenia Persons Smartt, *History of Eufaula, Alabama* (Privately published, 1930), 11-17.

28. Ibid.

29. "Eufaula Baptist Church, Minutes," 22 June 1837, archives, Samford University Library, Birmingham, Alabama.

30. William Tryon to Jesse Mercer, 17 September 1838, quoted in *The Christian Index,* 27 September 1838.

31. *The Christian Index,* 27 September 1838.

32. William Tryon to Jesse Mercer, 23 October 1838, quoted in *The Christian Index,* 8 November 1838.

33. *The Christian Index,* 8 November 1838.

34. "Eufaula Baptist Church Minutes," February 1839.

35. *The Christian Index,* 3 October 1839.

36. *Minutes of the Fifteenth Anniversary of the Baptist State Convention of Alabama Held at Grant's Creek Meeting House, Tuscaloosa County, Commencing on Saturday, November 10th, 1838* (Tuscaloosa: M. D. J. Slade at *The Monitor* Office, 1838), 10.

37. *Minutes of the Sixteenth Anniversary of the Baptist State Convention of Alabama Held at Oakmulgee Meeting House, Perry County, Commencing on Saturday, November 1st, 1839* (Tuscaloosa: M. D. J. Slade, 1839), 4.

38. Elizabeth Porter, *A History of Wetumpka* (Wetumpka, Ala.: Chamber of Commerce, 1957), 46.

39. J. D. Williams to W. C. Crane, 17 July 1838, William Carey Crane Papers, Texas Collection.

40. Porter, *A History of Wetumpka,* 53-54; Montgomery County Marriage License Records, Book E, 63. Montgomery, Alabama; *Minutes of the Sixteenth Anniversary of the Baptist State Convention of Alabama,* 16.

41. W. C. Crane to his wife, Alcesta Flora Crane, 9 June 1840, William Carey Crane Papers, Texas Collection.

42. *Eighteenth Anniversary of the Georgia Baptist Convention, Held at Richland, Twiggs County, Geo. On the 3rd, 4th & 6th days of May, 1839* (Washington: M. J. Kappal at the Office of *The Christian Index,* 1839), 4. Documents in the General Land Office, Austin, dated 10 May 1836, indicate

that a single man named William Tryon emigrated to the Republic of Texas in December 1835 and remained for a brief time. There is no evidence that this William Tryon and the William M. Tryon of this volume are the same, but this possibility does exist and may explain his interest in becoming a missionary to that country.

Chapter 2

1. *The Baptist Advocate,* 11 September 1841.

2. *The Christian Index,* 28 May 1841.

3. Morrell, *Flowers and Fruits,* 66.

4. Max Freund, trans., *Gustav Dresel's Houston Journal, Adventures in North America and Texas, 1837-1841* (Austin: University of Texas Press, 1954), 100.

5. *The Christian Index,* 28 May 1841.

6. Walter Prescott Webb, editor-in-chief, *The Handbook of Texas,* vol. 1. (Austin: The Texas State Historical Association, 1952), 875-76.

7. Samuel B. Hesler, *A History of Independence Baptist Church 1838-1969 and Related Organizations* (Dallas: Executive Board of the Baptist General Convention of Texas, 1970), 11.

8. Morrell, *Flowers and Fruits,* 77.

9. *The Baptist Advocate,* 11 September 1841.

10. Ibid.

11. *Baptist Banner and Western Pioneer,* 23 September 1841.

12. R. E. B. Baylor to James Huckins, 1 March 1859.

13. *Minutes of the Union Baptist Association held with the Oakland Church, Grimes County, Texas Commencing August 16th and ending August 19th, 1872* (Houston: Office of *The Texas Baptist Herald,* 1872), 26.

14. *Baptist Banner and Western Pioneer,* 16 September 1841.

15. *Baptist Banner and Western Pioneer,* 30 September 1841.

16. R. E. B. Baylor to James Huckins, 1 March 1859.

17. Ibid.

18. Link, *Texas Hist. and Bio. Magazine* 1:170.

19. Ibid.; William B. Sprague, *Annals of the American Pulpit; or Commemorative Notices of Distinguished American Clergymen of Various Denominations from the Early Settlement of the Country to the Close of the Year Eighteen Hundred and Fifty-Five with Historical Introductions,* vol. 6 (New York: Robert Carter & Brothers, 1860), 812-814.

20. *Baptist Banner and Western Pioneer,* 16 September 1841.

21. *The Christian Index,* 24 August 1841.

22. *Baptist Banner and Western Pioneer,* 14 October 1841.

23. Ibid.

24. Ibid.

25. *The Christian Index,* 24 August 1841; *Baptist Banner and Western Pioneer,* 16 September 1841.

26. *Baptist Banner and Western Pioneer,* 16 September 1841.

27. *The Christian Index,* 19 November 1841.

28. *The Christian Index,* 24 August 1841.

29. *The 10th Report of the American Baptist Home Mission Society, Presented by the Executive Committee at its Anniversary in New York, April 26, 1842, with the Treasurer's Report* (New York: American Baptist Home Mission Rooms, 1842), 31; American Baptist Home Mission Society, "Executive Committee Letter Book," 1841, 108.

30. *The Christian Index,* 25 February 1842.

Chapter 3

1. Seymour V. Connor, *Adventure in Glory* (Austin: Steck-Vaughn Company, 1965), 173-74.

2. *The Christian Index,* 1 October 1840.

3. Webb, ed. *Texas Handbook* 2:175.

4. *Baptist Banner and Western Pioneer,* 24 November 1842.

5. "Providence Baptist Church, Minutes," 7 May 1842, archives, The Southwestern Baptist Theological Seminary, Fort Worth, Texas.

6. *The Baptist Advocate,* 19 November 1842.

7. Ibid.

8. Joseph Milton Nance, *Attack and Counter-Attack, The Texas-Mexican Frontier, 1842* (Austin: University of Texas Press, 1964), 342.

9. *Journals of the Senate of the Seventh Congress of the Republic of Texas Convened at Washington on the 14th Nov., 1842* (Washington: Thomas Johnson, Public Printers, 1843), 9.

10. "Washington County, Tax Rolls," 1839-1845.

11. *Journals of the Senate of the Seventh Congress,* 101-102.

12. *The Religious Herald,* 21 December 1843.

13. Ibid.

14. Ibid.

15. "Washington County Tax Rolls"

16. Mary Putnam, *The Baptists and Slavery* (Ann Arbor, Mich.: George Wahr, Publishers, 1913), 21.

17. *Thirteenth Report of the American Baptist Home Mission Society Presented by the Executive Board at the Anniversary at Providence, Rhode Island, April 29, 1845* (New York: Baptist Home Mission Rooms, 1845), 45.

18. *Journals of Senate of the Eighth Congress of the Republic of Texas* (Houston: Cruger & Moore, Public Printers, 1844), 13-237: "Texas Senate Pay Voucher," 5 February 1844, Baylor University Subject Files, Pre-Foundation Events, William Tryon, Texas Collection.

19. *The Baptist,* 3 December 1844.

20. *The Christian Index,* 10 January 1845.

21. *The Religious Herald,* 28 November 1844.

22. Morrell, *Flowers and Fruits,* 208; *The Religious Herald,* 6 March 1845.

23. *The Christian Index,* 14 March 1845.

24. *Baptist Banner and Western Pioneer,* 28 November 1844.

Chapter 4

1. Sadie S. Conoway to S. P. Brooks, 8 November 1929, Samuel Palmer Brooks Papers, Texas Collection.

2. Frederick Eby, *The Development of Education in Texas* (New York: The MacMillan Company, 1925), 75.

3. H. P. N. Gammel, compiler, *The Laws of Texas 1822-1897,* vol. 2 (Austin: The Gammel Book Company, 1898), 134.

4. R. E. B. Baylor to James Huckins, 1 March 1859; "Minutes of the Second Annual Session of the Union Baptist Association Held at the Clear Creek Meeting House near Rutersvile in Western Texas Commencing on the 7th October A.D. 1841," Union Baptist Association Records, Texas Collection.

5. Ibid.

6. Ibid.

7. Several good discussions relating to the possible first officers and founding dates of the Texas Baptist Education Society are found in Link, *Texas Hist. and Bio. Magazine* 1:44; J. M. Carroll, *A History of Texas Baptists* (Dallas: Baptist Standard Publishing Co., 1923), 228-29; Harry Haynes, *The Life and Writings of Rufus C. Burleson Containing a Biography of Dr. Burleson by Hon. Harry Haynes* (Compiled and Published by Mrs. Georgia J. Burleson, 1901), 100-101; Morrell, *Flowers and Fruits,* 133, 138; Robert A. Baker, *Blossoming Desert, A Concise History of Texas Baptists* (Waco, Tex.: Word Books, 1970), 81-83; B. F. Fuller, *History of Texas Baptists* (Louisville, Ky.: Baptist Book Concern, 1900), 120-21; and James Huckins to the American Baptist Home Mission Society, 14 November 1841, quoted in *The Christian Index,* 21 January 1842.

8. Haynes, *Life and Writings,* 186.

9. A. H. Newman, *A Century of Baptist Achievement* (Philadelphia: American Baptist Publication Society, 1901), 337.

10. Baker, *Blossoming Desert,* 83.

11. Haynes, *Life and Writings,* 101.

12. Ibid.

13. R. E. B. Baylor correspondence, unaddressed and undated, R. E. B. Baylor Papers, Texas Collection; *Minutes of the Fifth Anniversary Meeting of the Union Baptist Association, Convened at Plum Grove Church, Fayette County, Texas, August 29th, 1844, and Days Following* (Washington: *The Vindicator* Office, 1844), 3.

14. R. E. B. Baylor to James Huckins, 1 March 1859.

15. *Journals of the Senate of the Ninth Congress of the Republic of Texas* (Washington: Miller & Cushney, Public Printers, 1845), 78.

16. Ibid., 90.

17. Ibid., 105.

18. Ibid., 108-109.

19. Ibid., 115

20. Ibid., 125.

21. R. E. B. Baylor to James Huckins, 1 March 1859.

22. *Journals of the House of Representatives of the Ninth Congress of the Republic of Texas* (Washington: Miller & Cushney, Public Printers, 1845), 181.

23. Ibid., 256, 261

24. Ibid., 299.

25. *The New York Recorder,* 24 July 1845.

26. "Baylor University Board of Trustee Minutes," Independence, Texas, 13 October 1845, Texas Collection.

27. Ibid.

28. Link, *Texas Hist. and Bio. Magazine,* 2:50.

29. *Telegraph and Texas Register,* 9 March 1842.

30. "Baylor University Trustees Minutes," 12-13 January 1846.

31. *The Texas Republican,* 13 December 1834, quoted in Arthur A. Grusendorf, "A Century of Education in Washington County, Texas." This is an article revised from Grusendorf's unpublished Ph.D. dissertation entitled "The Social and Philosophical Determinants of Education in Washington County since 1835" (University of Texas, 1938), 52.

32. Gammel, *Laws* 1:1295-1296.

33. Webb, ed., *Texas Handbook* 1:876

34. *Telegraph and Texas Register,* 28 January 1846.

35. Ibid., 14 October 1846.

36. "Minutes, Executive Committee, Georgia Baptist Convention," 16 March 1846.

37. *Proceedings of the First Triennial Meeting of the Southern Baptist Convention, Held at Richmond, Virginia, June 10, 11, 12, 13, & 15, 1846* (Richmond: H. K. Ellyson, 1846), 49-53; *The Southern Baptist Missionary Journal,* October 1846, 115.

38. *Telegraph and Texas Register,* 15 July 1846; *The Texas Presbyterian,* 16 January 1847.

39. *The Texas Presbyterian,* 16 January 1847.

Chapter 5

1. R. E. B. Baylor to James Huckins, 1 March 1859.

2. *The Southern Baptist Missionary Journal,* December 1846, 161; March 1847, 234-35.

3. Morrell, *Flowers and Fruits,* 144-45.

4. James Huckins to Benjamin H. Hill, 15 November 1841, quoted in *The Christian Index,* 21 January 1842.

5. Morrell, *Flowers and Fruits,* 146-47; R. E. B. Baylor correspondence, unaddressed and undated, indicates that this person was A. G. Haynes. J. M. Carroll, *A History,* 504-505, and several others report that this person was T. J. Jackson. All materials naming Jackson seem to rely upon Haynes, *Life and Writings,* 719, as the source.

6. *Minutes of a Called Session of the United Baptist Association Held at the Mt. Gilead Church, Washington County, Texas on Saturday, November 26th, 1842* (Washington: Thomas Johnson, 1843), 11.

7. *Minutes of the Fourth Anniversary Meeting of the Union Baptist Association Convened at Providence Church, Washington County, October 6, 1843 and Days Following* (Washington: Thomas Jackson Printers, 1844), 4.

8. *Minutes of the Fifth Anniversary Meeting of the Union Baptist Association Convened at Plum Grove Church, Fayette County, Texas, August 20, 1844 and Days Followiing* (Washington: *The Vindicator,* 1844), 14.

9. Ibid., 4.

10. Ibid., 13.

11. *The Twelfth Report of the American Baptist Home Mission Society Presented by the Executive Committee at its Anniversary in Philadelphia, April 23, 1844, with the Treasurer's Report* (New York: American Baptist Home Mission Rooms, 1844), 45; *The Thirteenth Report of the American Baptist Home Mission Society Presented by the Executive Committee at its Anniversary in Providence, Rhode Island, April 29, 1845, with the Treasurer's Report* (New York: American Baptist Home Mission Rooms, 1845), 37; *The Christian Index,* 21 January 1842.

12. *Minutes of the Sixth Anniversary Meeting of the Union Baptist Association Held with Mount Gilead Church, Washington County, Texas, Western Texas On the Ninth, Tenth, and Eleventh Days of October, 1845* (La Grange: *The Intelligencer* Office, 1845), 4.

13. *Minutes of the Seventh Annual Meeting of the Union Baptist Association Held with the Dove Church, Caldwell, Burleson County, on the 1st day of October, 1846 and Days Following,* n.p., n.d., 4.

14. Ibid., 17.

Chapter 6

1. R. E. B. Baylor to James Huckins, 1 March 1859.

2. *The Christian Index,* 11 February 1847.

3. *The Southern Baptist Missionary Journal,* July 1847, 49.

4. *Ibid.*

5. *The Texas Presbyterian,* 13 February 1847.

6. "Baylor University Trustees Minutes," 4 February 1847.

7. Ibid.

8. *Texas Baptist Herald,* 25 May 1899.

9. Ibid.

10. *The Southern Baptist Missionary Journal,* September 1847, 99.

11. "Baylor University Trustees Minutes," 27 April 1847.

12. *The Southern Baptist Missionary Journal,* September 1847, 100.

13. Ibid.

14. "Records of the First Baptist Church in Houston," 6 June 1847.

15. Ibid., 31 July 1847.

16. "Galveston Baptist Church, Minutes," 12 September 1847.

17. *Minutes of the Eighth Annual Meeting of the Union Baptist Association Held with the First Baptist Church in Houston, Texas, Commencing on Thursday, September 30, and Ending October 4, 1847,* n.p., n.d., 2.

18. Ibid., 6.

19. Ibid., 5.

20. Ibid., 11-12.

21. *The Christian Index,* 2 December 1847.

22. *The Texas Presbyterian,* 30 October 1847.

23. *Telegraph and Texas Register,* 18 November 1847.

24. Ibid.

25. *The Texas Presbyterian,* 16 October 1847.

26. Rufus C. Burleson to Sadie Clark, n.d., typescript in Baylor University Subject Files, Pre-Foundation Events, William Tryon, Texas Collection.

Cited References

BOOKS

History of the Baptist Denomination in Georgia: With a Biographical Compendium and Portrait Gallery of Baptist Ministers and Other Georgia Baptists. Atlanta: Compiled for *The Christian Index,* J. P. Harrison & Co. 1881.

Baker, Robert A. *The Blossoming Desert, A Concise History of Texas Baptists.* Waco, Tex.: Word Books, 1970.

Burleson, Georgia J., compiler. *The Life and Writings of Rufus C. Burleson, Containing a Biography of Dr. Burleson by Hon. Harry Haynes.* Privately Published, 1901.

Carroll, B. H., ed. *Standard History of Houston, Texas.* Knoxville, Tenn.: H. W. Crew & Co., 1912.

Connor, Seymour V. *Adventure in Glory.* Austin: Steck-Vaughn Company, 1965.

Dowell, Spright. *A History of Mercer University, 1833-1953.* Macon, Georgia: Mercer University, 1958.

Eby, Frederick. *The Development of Education in Texas.* New York: The MacMillan Company, 1925.

Freud, Max, trans. *Gustav Dresel's Houston Journal, Adventures in North America and Texas 1837-1841.* Austin: University of Texas Press, 1954.

Gammel, H. P. N., compiler. *The Laws of Texas 1822-1897,* vol. 2. Austin: The Gammel Book Company, 1898.

Hesler, Samuel B. *A History of Independence Baptist Church 1839-1969 and Related Organizations.* Dallas: Executive Board of the Baptist General Convention of Texas, 1970.

Link, J. B. *Texas Historical and Biographical Magazine.* Vols. 1 and 2. Austin, 1891.

Morrell, Z. N. *Flowers and Fruits from the Wilderness, or Thirty-Six Years in Texas and Two Winters in Honduras.* 1872. Reprint. Waco, Tex.: The Markham Press Fund of Baylor University Press, 1976.

Nance, Joseph Milton. *Attack and Counter-Attack, The Texas-Mexican Frontier, 1842.* Austin: University of Texas Press, 1964.

Newman, A. H. *A Century of Baptist Achievement.* Philadelphia: American Baptist Publication Society, 1901.

Porter, Elizabeth. *A History of Wetumpka.* Wetumpka, Ala.: Chamber of Commerce, 1957.

Putnam, Mary. *The Baptists and Slavery.* Ann Arbor, Mich.: George Wahr, 1913.

Schwitz, Joseph William. *Texas Statecraft 1836-1845.* San Antonio: The Naylor Company, 1941.

Smartt, Eugenia Persons. *History of Eufaula, Alabama.* Privately Published, 1930.

Sprague, William B. *Annals of the American Pulpit; or Commemorative Notices of Distinguished American Clergymen of various Denominations From the Early Settlement of the Country to the Close of the Year Eighteen Hundred and Fifty-five with Historical Introductions.* Vol. 6. New York: Robert Carter & Brothers, 1860.

Tryon, Wes M., ed. *The Tryon Family in America.* Wheaton, Md., 1960.

Webb, Walter Prescott, editor-in-chief. *The Handbook of Texas.* Vols. 1 and 2. Austin: The Texas State Historical Association, 1952.

NEWSPAPERS AND JOURNALS

The Baptist (Nashville, Tennessee), 3 December 1844.

The Baptist Advocate (New York), 11 September 1841; 19 November 1842.

Baptist Banner and Western Pioneer (Louisville, Kentucky), 16, 23, 30 September 1841; 14 October 1841; 24 November 1842; 28 November 1844.

The Christian Index (Penfield, Georgia), 27 September 1838; 8 November 1838; 3 October 1839; 14 May 1840; 28 May 1841; 24 August 1841; 19 November 1841; 21 January 1842; 25 February 1842; 10 January 1845; 14 March 1845; 11 February 1847; 2 December 1847; 25 December 1920.

The New York Register (New York), 24 July 1845.

The Religious Herald (Richmond, Virginia), 21 December 1843; 28 November 1844; 6 March 1845.

The Telegraph and Texas Register (Houston), 9 March 1842; 7, 28 January 1846; 15 July 1846; 14 October 1846; 18 November 1847.

Texas Baptist Herald (Houston), 25 May 1899.

The Texas Presbyterian (Houston), 16 January 1847; 13 February 1847; 16, 30 October 1847.

The Southern Baptist Missionary Journal (Richmond), October 1846; December 1846; March 1847, May 1847, July, 1847; September 1847.

LETTERS

Baylor, R. E. B., to James Huckins, 1 March 1859.

Conoway, Sadie, to S. P. Brooks, 8 November 1928.

Crane, W. C., to Alcesta Flora Crane, 9 June 1840.

Sanders, Billington, to Samuel Wait, 15 October 1833.

Williams, J. D., to W. C. Crane, 17 July 1838.

MINUTES AND PROCEEDINGS

Alabama Baptist Churches:

"Eufaula Baptist Church Minutes," 1837-1839

Alabama Baptist Convention:

Minutes of the Fifteenth Anniversary of the Baptist State Convention of Alabama Held at Grant's Creek Meeting House, Tuscaloosa County, Commencing on Saturday, November 10th, 1838. Tuscaloosa: M. D. J. Slade at the *Monitor* office, 1838.

American Baptist Home Mission Society:

The 10th Report of the American Baptist Home Missions Society, Presented by the Executive Committee at its Anniversary in New York, April 26, 1842, with the Treasurer's Report. New York: American Baptist Home Mission Rooms, 1842.

The Twelfth Report of the American Baptist Home Missions Society, Presented by the Executive Committee at its Anniversary in Philadelphia, April 23, 1844, with the Treasurer's Report. New York: American Baptist Home Mission Rooms, 1844.

The Thirteenth Report of the American Baptist Home Missions Society, Presented by the Executive Committee at its Anniversary in Providence, Rhode Island, April 29, 1845, with the Treasurer's Report. New York: American Baptist Home Mission Rooms, 1845.

Georgia Baptist Convention:

"Minutes," Executive Committee, Georgia Baptist Convention, 1836.

Minutes of the 14th Anniversary of the Georgia Baptist Convention, Held at Shiloh, Green County, 22-25 May, 1835. Washington, Ga.: Office of *The Christian Index,* 1836.

Minutes of the 15th Anniversary of the Georgia Baptist Convention, Held at Talbottom, Ga., 29-30 April and 2-3 May, 1836. Washington, Ga.: *Christian Index,* 1836.

Minutes of the Sixteenth Anniversary of the Georgia Baptist Convention, Held at Ruckersville, Georgia, on the 5th, 6th and 8th of May, 1837. Washington, Ga.: *The Christian Index,* 1837.

Eighteenth Anniversary of the Georgia Baptist Convention, Held at Richland, Twiggs County, Geo., on the 3d, 4th & 6th days of May, 1839.

Washington: M. J. Kappal at the Office of *The Christian Index,* 1839.

Southern Baptist Convention:

Proceedings of the First Triennial Meeting of the Southern Baptist Convention, Held at Richmond, Virginia, June 10, 11, 12, 13, & 15, 1846. Richmond: H. K. Ellyson, 1846.

Texas, Congress:

Journals of the House of Representatives of the Ninth Congress of the Republic of Texas. Washington: Miller & Cushney, Public Printers, 1849.

Journals of the Senate of the Seventh Congress of the Republic of Texas at Washington on the 14th Nov., 1842. Washington: Thomas Johnson, Public Printers, 1843.

Journals of the Senate of the Eighth Congress of the Republic of Texas. Houston: Crueger & Moore, Public Printers, 1844.

Journals of the Senate of the Ninth Congress of the Republic of Texas. Washington: Miller & Cushney, Public Printers, 1845.

Texas, Union Baptist Association:

"Minutes of the Second Annual Session of the Union Baptist Association held at the Clear Creek Meeting House near Rutersville in Western Texas Commencing on the 7th October A.D. 1841."

Minutes of a Called Session of the United Baptist Association Held at the Mt. Gilead Church, Washington County, Texas on Saturday, November 26th, 1842. Washington: Thomas Johnson, 1843.

Minutes of the Fourth Anniversary of the Union Baptist Association Convened at Providence Church, Washington County, October 6, 1843 and Days Following. Washington: Thomas Johnson, Printers, 1844.

Minutes of the Fifth Anniversary Meeting of the Union Baptist Association Convened at Plum Grove Church, Fayette County, Texas, August 29, 1844 and Days Following. Washington: *The Vindicator,* 1844.

Minutes of the Sixth Anniversary Meeting of the Union Baptist Association Held with Mount Gilead Church, Washington County, Texas, Western Texas on the Ninth, Tenth and Eleventh Days of October, 1845.

La Grange: Printed at *The Intelligencer* Office, 1845.

Minutes of the Seventh Annual Meeting of the Union Baptist Association, Held with the Dove Church, Caldwell, Burleson County, on the 1st day of October, 1846 and days following, n.p., n.d.

Minutes of the Eighth Annual Meeting of the Union Baptist Association Held with the First Baptist Church in Houston, Texas Commencing on Thursday, September 30, and Ending October 4, 1847, n.p., n.d.

Minutes of the Union Baptist Association held with the Oakland Church, Grimes County, Texas Commencing August 16th and Ending August 19th, 1872. Houston: Office of the *Texas Baptist Herald,* 1872.

Texas, Baptist Churches:

"Minutes," Galveston Baptist Church, 1840-1865.

"Minutes," Providence Baptist Church, 1842-1845.

Records of the First Baptist Church in Houston, 1841-1847.

Texas, Baylor University:

"Baylor University Board of Trustees Minutes," Independence, Texas, 1845-1886.

MISCELLANEOUS

American Baptist Home Mission Society, Executive Committee Letter Book, 1841.

Grusendorf, Arthur A. "A Century of Education in Washington County, Texas." Revised from "The Social and Philosophical Determinants of Education in Washington County since 1835." Ph.D. diss., University of Texas, 1938.

Mercer Institute, Account Book, 1833-1835.

Montgomery County Marriage License Record, Alabama, Book E, 63.

Washington County Tax Rolls, 1839-1845.

CPSIA information can be obtained at www.ICGtesting.com
Printed in the USA
BVOW020618050412

286926BV00001B/5/P

9 781602 585812